礼县旅游知识

INFORMATION ON TOURING TO LIXIAN

主　编　黄旭东
副主编　姚丽琴　杨启明　雷还州
　　　　张　藩　左世荣

西南交通大学出版社
·成都·

图书在版编目（CIP）数据

礼县旅游知识 = INFORMATION ON TOURING TO LIXIAN：汉英对照 / 黄旭东主编. 一成都：西南交通大学出版社，2019.11
ISBN 978-7-5643-7211-8

Ⅰ. ①礼… Ⅱ. ①黄… Ⅲ. ①旅游指南–礼县–汉、英 Ⅳ. ①K928.942.4

中国版本图书馆 CIP 数据核字（2019）第 247194 号

Lixian Lüyou Zhishi
礼县旅游知识
INFORMATION ON TOURING TO LIXIAN
主编　黄旭东

责任编辑	赵玉婷
助理编辑	吴启威
封面设计	曹天擎
出版发行	西南交通大学出版社 （四川省成都市金牛区二环路北一段 111 号 西南交通大学创新大厦 21 楼）
发行部电话	028-87600564　028-87600533
邮政编码	610031
网　　址	http://www.xnjdcbs.com
印　　刷	成都中永印务有限责任公司
成品尺寸	170 mm × 230 mm
印　　张	7.25
字　　数	131 千
版　　次	2019 年 11 月第 1 版
印　　次	2019 年 11 月第 1 次
书　　号	ISBN 978-7-5643-7211-8
定　　价	29.00 元

图书如有印装质量问题　本社负责退换
版权所有　盗版必究　举报电话：028-87600562

前　言

在这金风送爽、瓜果飘香的醉人季节,《礼县旅游知识》终于得以出版。它的面世会使更多的人了解礼县、建设礼县,将为礼县旅游事业的发展以及经济的发展起到不可估量的作用。《礼县旅游知识》的编写历经数年,它的出版有两个目的:其一是它可以作为一本宣传手册,帮助更多的国内外朋友了解礼县,了解她的人民,了解她的历史文化,了解她的环境和资源,为礼县引入更多投资;其二是它可以作为学生的课外阅读材料,使学生知道身边的东西如何用英文表达,培养学生学习外语的兴趣,增强学生学习外语的信心。因此,本书的编写力求用简单易懂的语言,让学生能够读懂,同时,也为他们更多地了解家乡提供资料。本书以中英双语形式从历史沿革、人口民族、社会经济、旅游景点、地方特产、风味小吃等几个方面对礼县做了全面的介绍,是一本帮助读者认识礼县、了解礼县的好书,也是一本进行爱国主义教育和提高学生外语学习兴趣的好教材。

旅游是为了了解祖国的大好河山和灿烂的历史文化,同时陶冶性情,从而受到启迪、获得自信、增强自尊。《礼县旅游知识》的宣传,吸引更多的人热爱礼县,把自己的聪明才智投入到建设礼县这一伟大的事业中来。从这一意义上来说,本书做了一项切实有益的工作。

本书由黄旭东策划并主笔,同时得到了礼县旅游局和礼县职业中等专业学校几位同志的大力支持和帮助。"赵世延家庙碑""文庙"等景点的中文部分由杨启明主笔。

本书的修订得到了天水师范学院 Tony 博士和王德安同志的帮助,在此一并表示衷心的感谢。

由于编者水平所限,书中错漏之处在所难免,恳请广大读者朋友批评和指正。

编　者

2019 年 8 月

Foreword

The refreshing autumn breeze caresses the land and the people, and the air is heavy with the aroma of melons and fruit. At this golden time, *Information on Touring to Lixian* comes into the world. Reading it will help more people know Lixian and come to construct it. It will make over-estimate contribution to the development of tourism and economy. We have spent years writing it to meet two different purposes. On the one hand, this book can be taken as a publicity book. As an advertisement brochure, it will help more people at home and abroad better understand the county, its people and cultures, its environments and resources, in order that they may invest in Lixian. The products that become famous and the natural resources may provide you with useful information for your commercial and business interests. On the other hand, it can be a reading book outside class, students at school will know more about their hometown before they graduate from schools. They will learn how to talk about things around them in English. Especially, it may arouse their interest and build up their confidence for the students who are not doing well in the English study. It is necessary that teachers try to bring English-teaching far closer into the actual and real life. In view of this, the book is written in simple and easy English. In this book Lixian has been introduced to readers, including its historical evolution, population and nationalities, economy and society, scenic spots, as well as local products and snacks. It is a good book not only for readers to know Lixian but also for teachers to improve the students' interest in studying English.

Traveling is to learn our motherland, such as beautiful mountains, rivers and brilliant history civilization. At the same time, it can also shape people's temperament, acquire self-confidence, strengthen self-respect, attract more people to love Lixian passionately, and put their own intelligence and ability to the great undertaking of developing Lixian. At this point, this book will make beneficial work.

This book was scripted by Huang Xudong, who wrote most of the contents, and the Tourism Bureau of Lixian offered a great deal of help. Several English teachers in Lixian Vocational and Technical School offered strong support. Here I express my heartfelt thanks to them.

Comrade Wang De'an, and Doctor Tony in Tianshui Normal College, offered help to the correction of this book. I express my thanks as well.

But because of my limited knowledge, the mistakes are hard to avoid, I hope readers will try to inform us. At the same time, I hope it will be a pleasure to read this book and I wish you a happy and fruitful journey!

The Author
August ,2019

目 录

第一章 礼县概况 1
  1. 概 览 1
  2. 位置・人口・民族 2
  3. 历史沿革 3
  4. 社会・经济・资源 5

第二章 主要旅游景点 7
  1. 大堡子山秦公陵园 7
  2. 秦西垂博物馆 8
  3. 祁山诸葛亮庙 8
  4. 卤城盐井祠 10
  5. 大香山生态风景区 11
  6. 铁笼山——三国古战场遗址 11
  7. 洮坪原始森林游览区 12
  8. 大河边草原风情游览区 12
  9. 红河水库度假区 13
  10. 翠峰观生态风景区 13
  11. 黄金寺 13
  12. 太平山公园 14
  13. 苗河水库度假区 14
  14. 赵世延家庙碑 14
  15. 文 庙 15
  16. 赤土山园林 15
  17. 王仁裕神道碑 16
  18. 新中川烈士陵园 16
  19. 高寺头遗址 17

20. 石碑下遗址 17
21. 瑶峪墓群 17
22. 城隍庙 18
23. 红军墓 18

第三章　地方工农业产品 20
1. 苹　果 20
2. 八盘梨 20
3. 大　蒜 21
4. 柿　子 21
5. 石　榴 21
6. 花　椒 21
7. 烟　叶 22
8. 王坝豆腐 23
9. 松花蜜 23
10. 核桃麦芽糖 23
11. 核　桃 24
12. 青铜器仿制品 24
13. 地方酒 24

第四章　山野菜 26
1. 羊肚菌 26
2. 蕨　菜 26
3. 苦芥菜 27
4. 木龙头 27

第五章　中药材 29
1. 大　黄 29
2. 黄　芪 30
3. 柴　胡 30
4. 甘　草 30
5. 当　归 31
6. 党　参 31

第六章　地方小吃 33
1. 热面皮 33

  2. 猪油饼 ··· 33
  3. 饸饹面 ··· 34
  4. 臊子面 ··· 34
  5. 肉夹馍 ··· 34
  6. 酒　醅 ··· 34
  7. 宽川凉粉 ··· 35
  8. 烧　烤 ··· 35
  9. 盐官扁食 ··· 35
  10. 永兴扯面 ·· 36
第七章　补充资料 ··· 37
  1. 珍奇鱼种——娃娃鱼 ·· 37
  2. 礼县县名考 ··· 37
  3. 县　城 ··· 37
  4. 汉代祭天遗址 ··· 38
  5. 礼县古八景 ··· 39
  6. 民间传说 ··· 41
  7. 新闻报道 ··· 44
参考文献 ·· 102

CONTENTS

Chapter One Introduction of Lixian ·················· 48
  1. A Brief Survey of Lixian ······················· 48
  2. Position, Population and Nationalities ·············· 50
  3. Historical Evolution ·························· 51
  4. Society, Economy and Resources ·················· 52

Chapter Two Scenic Spots ························ 53
  1. Dabuzi Mountain's Qingongs' Funerary Park ·········· 53
  2. Xichui Museum of the Qin Dynasty in Lixian ·········· 55
  3. Zhuge Liang Temple at Qi Mountain ················ 55
  4. Ancestral Temple over the Salt Well ················ 58
  5. An Ecological Scenic Spot of the Great Fragrant Mountain (Xiangshan) ································· 59
  6. Ancient Battleground-Tielong Mountain ············· 60
  7. Forest Region of Taoping ······················· 61
  8. Grasslands of Dahebian ························ 62
  9. Honghe Reservoir ···························· 62
  10. An Ecological Scenic Spot of the Emerald Mount Temple ··· 62
  11. Golden Temple ······························ 63
  12. Taiping Mountain Park ························ 64
  13. Miaohe Reservoir ···························· 64
  14. Ancestral Temple Stele of Zhao Shiyan ············· 65
  15. Confucius' Temple ··························· 65
  16. Red Mountain Garden ························ 66
  17. Stone Tablet of Wang Renyu ···················· 66
  18. New Zhongchuan Martyrs' Mausoleum ·············· 67

19. Gaositou Relic ·· 69
　20. Shibeixia Relic ··· 69
　21. A Cluster of Tombs in Yaoyu ································ 69
　22. Chenghuang Temple ··· 70
　23. Red Army Tombs ·· 70
Chapter Three　Famous Local Industrial and
　　　　　　　　Agricultural Products ······························ 71
　1. Apples ·· 71
　2. Bapan Pears ··· 71
　3. Garlic ·· 72
　4. Persimmons ··· 72
　5. Pomegranates ··· 73
　6. Wild Pepper (Chinese Prickly Ash) ·························· 73
　7. Tobacco ··· 74
　8. Wangba Tofu ··· 74
　9. Songhua Honey ·· 75
　10. Malt Sugar with Walnut Kernels ···························· 75
　11. Walnut ··· 76
　12. Imitation Bronzes ··· 76
　13. Local Alcoholic beverages ··································· 76
Chapter Four　Wild Vegetables ····································· 78
　1. Yangdu Vegetable ·· 78
　2. Bracken ··· 78
　3. Kujie Vegetable ·· 79
　4. Buds of Mulong Tree ·· 79
Chapter Five　Traditional Medicinal Herbs ······················· 80
　1. Rhubarb ··· 80
　2. Milk Vetch ·· 81
　3. Chinese Thorowax Root ······································ 81
　4. Licorice ··· 82
　5. Angelica Root ·· 82
　6. Codonopsis Pilosula ··· 83

Chapter Six   Local Snacks ································ 84
    1. Hot Starch Noodles ································ 84
    2. Lard Cakes ································ 84
    3. Buckwheat Heluo Noodles ································ 85
    4. Saozi Noodles ································ 85
    5. Unleavened Bread with Pork ································ 85
    6. Sweet Fermented Wheat ································ 86
    7. Kuanchuan Jelly ································ 86
    8. Various Baked or Roast Delicacy ································ 86
    9. Yan guan Dumplings ································ 87
    10. Yongxing Pulled Noodles ································ 87
Chapter Seven   Supplementary Reading ································ 88
    1. A Rare Kind of Fish—Giant Salamander ································ 88
    2. Examination of Lixian County's Name ································ 88
    3. Lixian County Seat ································ 89
    4. Sites of Heaven Worship in the Han Dynasty ································ 90
    5. The Ancient Eight Scenes in Lixian County ································ 90
    6. Folklore ································ 91
    7. News Report ································ 95
References ································ 102

第一章 礼县概况

1. 概　览

礼县，古称西垂、西犬丘、兰仓，地处甘肃省东南部，陇南市北部。礼县历史悠久、文化灿烂、山川秀美、资源丰富，素有"秦人发祥地，三国古战场"之美誉。

礼县，是一片古老而神奇的沃土。已发掘的文化遗址证明，早在六千多年前的新石器时代晚期，我们的祖先就在这里繁衍生息，创造了灿烂的历史文明，而且由于特殊的地理位置，长江巴蜀文化和黄河仰韶文化在这里交汇。悠久的历史孕育了礼县独具特色的仰韶、先秦、三国等历史文化；也造就了东汉辞赋家赵壹，五代诗人王仁裕，元代重臣赵世延，明代礼部尚书门克新等一大批历史名人；同时也为这片古老的土地留下了众多的名胜古迹，其中最为著名的有：大堡子山秦公第一陵园——秦西垂陵园，全国五大武侯祠之一——祁山武侯祠，诗圣杜甫流寓秦州时留下的《盐井诗》中描绘的卤城盐井祠和姜维与司马昭交战之地——铁笼山等。

在这片约4 300平方千米的土地上，养育着52万多人。礼县不仅拥有灿烂的文化，而且拥有丰富的自然资源，境内铨水所产的大黄素有"中国大黄甲天下，铨水大黄最盛名"之美称，20世纪80年代，礼县大黄出口量占全国的56%。礼县也是全国32处优质苹果生产基地之一和"甘肃八梨"之一——八盘梨的重要产区。苹果种植面积达30多万亩[①]，年产优质苹果20万吨以上。位于礼县西北部的洮坪乡金山村、罗坝乡李坝村之间30千米长的山脉为礼县金矿带，已探明纯金储量10 000千克，远景储量50 000千克以上，黄金生产为礼县龙头产业。礼县的花椒颗粒浑圆，香气浓郁，油脂丰富，因色鲜红，俗称"大红袍"，为饮食中的上等调料。

---

① 1亩约等于666.7平方米。

宽川的大麻具有色泽光亮白净，纤维绵软细长，韧性好，耐磨损，透气性好，吸湿性佳等优点。另外，还有苦芥菜、蕨菜、羊肚菜、松花蜜等土特产品。

　　礼县气候四季分明，年平均气温 9 ℃，许多植物均能生长，小麦、玉米、土豆、大豆为当地主要农作物，这里生长的烟叶也很有名。矿产资源以金矿、银矿最为丰富。由于气候温和、雨水充沛，境内森林有 125 万亩，森林覆盖率为 21%；草原面积达 170 万亩，畜牧业发达，年成交大牲畜数十万头。著名的盐官骡马市场为西北最大的骡马市场。

　　改革开放以来，勤劳淳朴的礼县人民在党的政策指引下，自力更生，艰苦创业，礼县的经济和社会各项事业迅猛发展，特别是交通、通讯、电力等基础设施日趋完善，教育、卫生、贸易、旅游事业不断发展，城镇化水平不断提高，全县国民经济综合实力不断增强。在坚持农业特色产业基础地位的同时，黄金矿产、地方工业、贸易旅游已成为当地经济的主体。一、二、三产业均衡发展的格局已初步形成。展望未来，随着西部大开发战略的进一步实施，通过勤劳智慧的礼县儿女的艰苦奋斗和社会各界有识之士的团结协作，有着辉煌历史的礼县，必将迎来璀璨的明天。

2. 位置·人口·民族

　　礼县地处甘肃省东南部，陇南市北部，距省会兰州 345 千米，北界甘谷、武山，南临武都，东连天水、西和，西接宕昌、岷县。气候温和，适宜发展农业和畜牧业。

　　礼县位于北纬 33°35′–34°31′，东经 104°37′–105°36′之间。西起上坪乡的没遮拦梁，东至盐官镇的罗堡村，长 88 千米；南起三峪乡的白马石，北至固城乡的庄子河，长 103 千米。全县总面积 4 299.92 平方千米，占全省总面积的 0.947%。

　　礼县地势西北向东南倾斜，平均海拔 1 825 米。西南系岷山山脉，山大沟深，森林茂密；东北为秦岭山脉，土地肥沃，山川适宜耕作。县内最高峰为没遮拦梁，海拔 3 312 米，凤凰咀、八盘山、牛顶山、大山、洒风地、铁家山、尖草山、金灵山属于岷山山系；正字山、店子岭、见山寺、齐寿山、白草山、雷王山、香山等属于秦岭山系。境内有"一水十河"，即西汉水、峁水河（红河）、漾水河（西和河）、永坪河、燕子河、谷峪河、洮坪河、碧玉河、邓家河、清水河和太石河。西汉水共纳14条长年河和季节河，纵贯全境，汇入嘉陵江。气候属暖温带大陆性季风气候，冬季寒冷干燥，夏季炎热多雨，年平均气温9.9℃，1月平均气温-3℃，7月平均气温21.4℃，年降水量500.2毫米，无霜期183天，年平均日照时数1 968.1小时。

以县城为起点，东至县界——罗家堡村33千米，自界至天水33千米。北至县界——李家台子北梁37千米，自界至甘谷县城27千米；西至县界——木树关北的分水岭30千米，自界至武山县城36千米，西至县界——黄沙子梁48千米，自界至岷县城60千米；西南至县界——沙金43千米，自界至宕昌县城39千米，南至县界——草坪69千米，自界至武都区30千米，东至县界——永兴乡15千米，自界至西和县城21千米。

礼县现辖34乡2镇，总人口约53万人，有汉族、回族、满族、藏族、蒙古族、土家族等六个民族，其中汉族人口占98%。

3. 历史沿革

礼县境内，气候温和、土地肥沃，河流、森林、山川纵横，具有生存和繁衍的条件。据考，几千年前，就有古人类在这一带劳动、繁衍、生息。现已发现属于原始社会氏族公社新石器时期的仰韶文化和先秦文化的遗址。具有悠久历史的礼县，被称为"秦人发祥地"。它的演变大体经历是：夏、商时（前2100—前1100）为氐人、羌人居住地；秦朝时（前221—前206），属于陇西郡西县；三国时期（220—280），东北部属于魏国天水郡之西县，西南部属于蜀国武都郡之武都县；北魏时（386—534），属于南秦州汉阳郡之兰仓；北宋时（960—1127），分属于岷州长道县、大潭县；明成化九年（1473）开始设置礼县，属于巩昌府秦州。

礼县，1949年8月17日解放，归属于武都专区管辖。1955年，归属于天水专区管辖。1958年8月，礼县与西和县合并为西礼县。1962年

1月撤销西礼县，恢复原建制。1985年6月又划归陇南地区。

历史沿革的详细资料如下：

石桥乡高寺头仰韶文化遗址，1964年出土人首器形盖，1986年又出土了石、陶、骨器多件，经测定系距今五千多年前氏族公社时期的物品。夏、商时期，它属于雍州。大禹"墦冢导漾"，导的就是流经礼县境内的西汉水。周朝时期，周孝王"邑非子于秦"之前，秦人的发祥地"西垂（西犬丘）"就在礼县东北的永兴一带。"非子邑秦"后，虽然秦都邑短时间地迁到了今清水县境内的秦亭。但很快秦庄公又将都邑迁回"西垂"，"居其故西犬丘。"秦昭襄王时设置陇西郡，管辖礼县一部分地域。秦朝时，地域东北部属于陇西郡的西县，西南部仍为氐、羌人居住，没有设置郡县。西汉时，地域东北部属于凉州刺史部陇西郡的西县，西南部属于益州刺史部武都郡的嘉陵道和陇西郡的羌道，王莽改西县为西治。东汉时，东北部属于凉州刺史部汉阳郡的西县，西南部属于武都郡的武都县及羌道。三国时期，东北部属于秦州汉阳郡的西县隶属于魏，西南部属于武都郡的武都县隶属于蜀。晋朝时期，东北部属于秦州天水郡的始昌县（晋改西县为始昌），西南部属于武都郡的武都县。仇池国（296—322）时期，全部地域属于仇池国。前赵（304—329）、后赵（319—351）、前凉（314—376）、前秦（351—394）、后秦（384—417）时期，这几个地方割据的政权或全部或部分占据过礼县地域。其间，东北部均称天水郡始昌县；西南部均称仇池郡。前凉时期，曾在东北部设置西城校尉。西秦（385—431）时期，东北部属于秦州汉阳郡的阳廉县，西南部分属于仇池郡及白马郡。北魏时期，红河、盐官一带分别属于秦州汉阳郡的阳廉、黄瓜二县。永兴、平泉一带分别属于南秦州天水郡的水南、平泉、平原三县，城关地区属于南秦州汉阳郡的兰仓、谷泉二县，江口以下地区分别属于南秦州仇池郡的阶陵、仓泉二县。西魏时期，盐官以东地区仍属于秦州天水郡阳廉、黄瓜二县，永兴、城关地区分别属于成州汉阳郡的水南、汉阳二县，西南部地区分别属于成州潭水郡的潭水、甘若、武宝、相山四县及成州仇池郡的阶陵、仓泉二县。北周时，盐官以东属于黄瓜县，永兴、城关地区属于成州仇池郡汉阳县，西南部地区属于成州仇池郡的潭水、上禄二县。唐朝时期，东北部先属于山南西道成州的汉源、长道二县，后属于陇右道秦州的长道县，西南部分属于陇右道成州的上禄县及宕州的良宫县。盐官城曾为党项马邑州治所，隶属于秦州都督府。五代的岐、唐、晋、周时期，东北部属于陇右道秦州天雄、雄武节度使所管辖的长道县，西南部没于吐蕃。五代时全县地域没于吐蕃。北宋时，东北部属于长道县，西南部属于属大潭县，两县先属秦凤路的秦州、后改属岷州。南宋时期，仍为长道、大潭两县地，但改属于利州西路的西和州所辖，盐官以东地域属于天水军（州级建制，治所在今天的天水镇）辖治。元朝时，东北部的长道县地域并入西和州，而于今城关镇别置"礼店、文州蒙古汉军西番军民元帅府"，下辖"礼店、文州蒙古汉军西番军民上千户所"及"礼店、汉州蒙古军民奥鲁千户所"；元帅府负责西和州、武阶、文州地区的军民安全，"上千户所"则仅统摄今天的城关及西南部地域的军民。明朝初期继承了元朝的建制，洪武四年（1371）置"礼店守御千户所"隶属于岷州卫，属陕西都司，洪武十五年（1382）改隶属于秦州卫。明成化九年（1472）割秦州十九里设置礼县，属巩昌府所领的秦州管辖，原"千户所"与县并存不废。清朝时期，顺治十六年（1659）裁撤卫所十百户，将巩昌卫、文县所、西固所归并礼县统辖，属于巩昌府。清雍正六年（1727）改属于秦州。民国二年（1913）袁世凯令各州府改道，礼县属于陇南道，旋改渭川道。民国十六年（1927）废除道，县直属于省。民国二十五年（1936）蒋介石令甘肃全省设七个行政专员公署，礼县属第四区（天水）专署管辖。1949年8月17日礼县解放，隶属于武都专区，1955年10月划归天水专区，1985年7月归陇南地区，2004年7月属陇南市。

4. 社会·经济·资源

礼县土地面积宽广，气候适宜，是一个以种植业为主的农业县，主要粮食作物有小麦、玉米、土豆、大豆等，经济作物有胡麻、油菜、烟叶等，经济林有苹果、核桃、花椒等。现在已经发展为以农业为主，以地方中小工业和第三产业为辅助产业的县。除农业之外，礼县政府也重视林业、牧业、工业和旅游业。随着改革开放和西部大开发战略的实施，礼县的经济和社会各项事业都得到了长足的发展；现代化进程进一步加快，教育、科学技术、文化、卫生事业均取得了显著的发展；交通、通信、电力等基础设施日趋完善；人民的物质和文化生活水平日益提高；城镇化水平不断提升；产业结构日趋合理；已迈出由资源、人口大县向旅游、经济大县转变的坚定步伐。

礼县资源丰富，有六大资源优势：一是以黄金矿为代表的矿产资源优势；二是以铨水大黄为代表，包括大黄、黄芪、柴胡、甘草、当归等在内的中药材资源优势；三是以大河边草原为基础的畜牧业资源优势；四是以苹果、花椒为代表的林果资源优势；五是巨大的水能资源优势；六是以先秦、三国文化为依托的旅游资源优势。

思考与实践

1. 礼县的历史文化有什么特点？为什么？
2. 礼县有哪些著名土特产品？礼县的土特产品说明礼县的经济发展存在什么问题？
3. 礼县的地势特点是什么？最高峰是什么？
4. 礼县境内有哪些主要河流？在历史进程中西汉水曾对礼县的经济和文化起何作用？
5. 礼县四面分别与哪几个县相邻？
6. 礼县的气候特点怎样？适宜于哪些作物生长？
7. 礼县的历史沿革说明，这片土地打下了先辈们奋斗的烙印，饱含了他们图强的血汗。我们既然懂得了历史，就应该热爱生我养我的土地，同时关注礼县的前途和未来。谈一谈自己准备为家乡的建设做点什么。
8. 县城是否是礼县政治、经济、文化中心？你认为礼县的飞速发展，存在着怎样的危机？
9. 礼县的优势资源是什么？它们对礼县经济的发展有何作用？

第二章 主要旅游景点

1. 大堡子山秦公陵园

礼县，古之"西垂、西犬丘"，秦人最早的都邑所在地。据《史记·秦本纪》记载：秦人先祖"在西戎，保西垂""非子居犬丘""庄公居其西犬丘""秦仲、庄公、襄公葬西垂"。西垂或是西犬丘，是秦人走向中原、成就霸业的摇篮。

另据《史记·秦本纪》记载，秦人属于嬴姓，源于山东，殷商末年，嬴人首领一路进攻，进到渭水中游一带，守卫商王朝的边疆。随着周王朝取代商王朝，嬴人守卫的地区也被周人占领，在其首领大骆的带领下，沿渭水西进，继续寻找生存之地，最后迁移到渭河以南，远离周人中心的西汉水上游地区，即现在礼县的东部一带，从而保持了相对的独立，为以后的发展壮大奠定了基础。在这里，他们战胜了力量相对弱小的氐人，修建了城邑。周王朝建立后，他们归顺了周王朝，周天子认可他们占据"西犬丘"，确立了他们的社会地位。秦人先祖——非子善于养马，受到周孝王的赏识，封为附庸，邑之秦，此后，非子的儿子秦仲被封为大夫，秦仲在对戎作战中死后，其子庄公继承遗志对戎作战，并收复领地，被宣王封为西垂大夫。庄公次子襄公在平定叛乱中，曾护送周平王迁都洛邑，因有功被封为诸侯，正式立国。庄公死后，文公继承王位，继续对戎作战，占领了陕西岐山地区，完全结束了游牧生活，开始了农耕生活，社会制度也随之由原始社会进入奴隶社会，成为真正意义上的国家。秦人的发展壮大始终未摆脱"西垂"这一中心。

20世纪90年代初，在位于礼县城东12千米处的大堡子山发掘出土四座规模宏大的秦公墓，出土的文物全国独一无二，闻名海内外，其中国家一级保护文物达300余件，专家对出土文物进行分析研究后，初步认定其或是秦仲，或是庄公，或是襄公的陵墓，并确立了此陵园为秦第一陵园的地位，称之为"西垂陵园"。秦公墓的开掘，揭开了"西垂陵园"和"秦人发祥地"这两大千年谜团，也证实了《史记》中的相关记载的真实性，引起了史学界和考古界的巨大轰动。夏、商、周断代工程专家李学勤先生指出："礼县为秦人发祥之地，关系中国古代史文化甚为深巨……有裨益于考古界，及历史学研究的进程。"陕西文物考古所副所长曹玮说："本世纪甘肃文物考古有两大发现，一是敦煌藏经洞，二是礼县大堡子山秦公墓。"

大堡子山"秦公陵园"的保护开发已引起社会各界的普遍关注，开发规划已由陕西省古建筑设计研究院设计完成，并通过专家的评审。在不远的将来，秦西垂陵园将再现其原始风貌，供海内外学者、游人、修学考古、参观游览。

2. 秦西垂博物馆

秦西垂博物馆，现指礼县博物馆，位于县城西大街文化娱乐中心院内，以其所收藏的稀世之宝而闻名，馆内共收藏历代文物 3 000 余件，分为 15 种类型，即化石、炻器、骨器、陶器、瓷器、铜器、铁器、玉器、金银器、古钱币、砖刻、木刻、书画、史料。国家一级保护文物 100 余件，其余为省级和县级保护文物，是一处研究仰韶、先秦、三国等文化的宝库。2000 年，一些文物在北京大学成功展出，引起了国内外历史学家、考古学家的普遍关注。目前，计划投资 1 400 多万元，占地 54 亩的新的秦西垂博物馆正在修建，在近年内可接待越来越多的国内外游客。

3. 祁山诸葛亮庙

祁山诸葛亮庙或称武侯祠。祁山，东起盐官，西至大堡子山，位于西汉水北侧，绵延 25 千米，地扼蜀、陇之咽喉，地势控制着攻守之要冲，是三国时祁山古战场的天然屏障，常为蜀、魏必争之地。三国时著名政治家、军事家诸葛亮"六出祁山"的故事，随着电视剧《三国演义》的播出而家喻户晓，祁山诸葛亮庙也名声大振。

建兴五年（227）三月，诸葛亮在成都向后主——刘禅上书《出师表》后，进入汉中设临时丞相府。建兴六年（228）四月，诸葛亮一出祁山，街亭一战失利，诸葛亮挥泪斩马谡；是年冬天，诸葛亮二出祁山，围住陈仓，因粮草不济而退兵；建兴七年（229），三出祁山，蜀将陈式占领了武都、阴平，诸葛亮到达建威城（今西和县内）；建兴八年（230），诸葛亮四出祁山，蜀将魏延从西面攻入天水、陇南的羌氐一带，大败魏将郭淮；建兴九年（231），诸葛亮五出祁山，破上邽，李严谎报，"军事无非是粮"，诸葛亮撤兵；建兴十二年（234），诸葛亮六出祁山，10万蜀军杀出斜谷口，屯兵五丈原，八月诸葛亮卒于军中。事实上诸葛亮只在建兴六年、建兴九年两次到达祁山，另有两次接近祁山，还有两次未到祁山。六出祁山是指诸葛亮晚年的整个北伐战略行动，也是诸葛亮"鞠躬尽瘁，死而后已"精神的象征。

祁山堡位于祁山地区中部，西汉水北岸，是一座石基土填的孤峰，四周不粘不连，状如乌龟又似战舰，诸葛亮庙建在峰顶。相传两晋伊始，堡上即建有诸葛亮庙，人们四时祭祀，热闹非凡。祁山诸葛亮庙是千年后保存下来的全国五大武侯祠之一。

来到祁山，忽见一峰突起，四面如削，高数十丈，犹如茫茫大海中的一叶孤舟，万里平原上的一座丘陵。游客步入祁山堡的堡门后，沿着小道拾级而上，道路两侧建有展室，展室中有名人字画及国内外名人的留影。当游客爬上祁山堡顶，首先映入眼帘的是悬挂于大门之上由"陇上书法泰斗"——顾子惠题写的"武侯祠"匾额，前后《出师表》碑文镶嵌在门两侧的墙上，睹物思人，诸葛亮"不忘先帝知遇之恩，为兴复蜀汉鞠躬尽瘁、死而后已的伟大形象"跃然眼前。进入院内，有始建于两晋，重建于明清的孔明殿、关羽殿、起佛殿一进三院。塑于道光年间的诸葛亮像，虽是木胎泥塑，却金装彩绘、造型精致、比例协调、神态自然。诸葛亮手执羽扇、栩栩如生地坐在大殿中央。前院两边有跟随诸葛亮领兵征战祁山的文武将长廊，这些翔实生动的图画，具有很高的历史价值和艺术价值。另外，庙内陈列的题词和碑刻众多，有匾额30多面，对联近10副，碑刻20余通。其中，明万历七年（1579）所立的，浙江道监察御史郑国仕题《登祁山谒武侯祠》碑、清光绪年间王化南草书其师之诗文《祁山远眺》等碑文为游人所敬慕，具有极高的文学价值和书法价值。

　　游客站在祁山堡的顶上，极目四望，昔日古战场尽收眼底。东北有天水关、盐井祠、木门道、九古堆"长蛇阵"；南面有当年埋藏伏兵的"圈马沟"和"藏兵湾"。相传堡上有一天然古洞，直通西汉水畔，是当时蜀军汲水之道。传说诸葛亮当年巡逻军营时，也是从此洞出入。西汉水河心有块巨石，是诸葛亮的上马石。游客瞻仰先烈的遗址，回顾历史，仿佛置身于昔日战场，惊险而神奇，苍茫而悠远。

4. 卤城盐井祠

　　盐官，古称卤城，历史悠久，是礼县东大门，也是礼县的第一重镇。位于盐官镇南门外骡马市场附近的盐井，发掘于周朝秦人占据时期。战国时，秦国在此地设立官府管理盐业生产，历代相承、营煮不辍，久而久之官名易为地名。井盐生产从它被发掘到中华人民共和国成立后，一直是当地人民的重要的手工业，也是他们主要的经济来源。20世纪50年代，本地的"盐民"多达300余户，年生产食盐达40多万千克，盛况空前，煮盐的青烟弥漫于整个平川。

　　《史记·秦本纪》记载："非子居犬丘，好马及畜，善养息之。犬丘人言之周孝王，孝王召使马于汧渭之间，马大蕃息。"非子善于养马，得到了周孝王的赏识，让他继承了祖先——伯益的"嬴"姓，号称秦嬴邑之秦。"马大蕃息"除了说明秦人牧马有方和西汉水流域水草丰茂外，盐官一带遍地流淌的卤水更是起了不小的作用。因马长期饮用卤水，膘肥体壮，毛色发亮，故而盐官一带所产的"骡马"驰名全国，今日，盐官骡马市场已成为西北第一骡马市场。

　　盐官生产的盐还具有一定的药理作用，《读史方舆纪要》记述其盐能"瘘瘤"。今天当地人民依然用盐水洗浴治疗关节炎等疾病，疗效非凡。盐井祠现存发掘于周朝的盐井一口，口方三尺八寸，深五丈一尺[①]，盐水仍不断向外涌流，煮盐全套工具保存完好。唐代以来的文人墨客所留碑文墨迹，为盐井祠增加了史学和文学研究价值，其中以唐朝大诗人杜甫

　　[①] 1丈约等于3.3米，1尺约等于0.33米，1寸约等于0.033米。

入川途经盐官时所留《盐井诗》最为著名。

盐神庙一进三院，供奉着"盐婆婆"，在漳县的盐川镇也有一处盐井，供奉的神为"盐爷爷"。据说每隔几年漳县盐井就不产盐了，当地人打趣地说，盐婆婆与盐爷爷在约会，盐爷爷把盐也带走了。用这种盐"点制"的豆腐，鲜嫩、酥脆、色亮、味香，品尝一次令人回味无穷，久久难忘。

盐官盐井作为当时社会经济文化遗址，与先秦文化的产生与发展是密不可分的，秦人对西垂包括对盐井的开发，为秦国的发展壮大奠定了经济基础。相信在不远的将来，盐文化作为先秦文化的组成部分必将走出礼县，走向世界。

5. 大香山生态风景区

大香山生态风景区位于礼县县城南 50 千米的礼县、西和县交界处，海拔 2 532 米。据《香山传》记载，香山为兴林国的妙庄王的三女儿——妙善修仙成道之处，自古名刹荟萃，规模宏大。早在大汉初年，这里就是道教活动的圣地，历代均有增补。

香山是礼县境内的一座山峰，这里过去山野苍茫，松柏参天，但 1958 年时被破坏，从 1982 年开始，礼县与西和县实施了飞播计划，又连续进行点播、撒播和补植，如今已经成林 26 万亩。1983 年，庙宇也得以修缮。山上现有许多景点，如老虎洞、悄悄泉、点头树、冰凌洞、姐妹石、舍身崖等。每年的农历四月初八到五月初五，游客纷沓而至，名刹道观给人以仙境之感。

每年的农历四月初八是香山庙会，也是游香山的最好时机，这时的香山春光灿烂，山清水秀，风和日丽，花香鸟语，彩蝶纷飞，游人从四面八方蜂拥而来，庙内香烟缭绕，庙外小商贩的吆喝不断，道家、佛门清静之地一下子热闹非凡，充满生气。

6. 铁笼山——三国古战场遗址

铁笼山，位于礼县县城西南 15 千米处。沿"石草公路"南行，远望有一山崛起，绝壁峭峙，云高孤险，状若悬壶。西汉水绕其阴，急流翻滚，两岸峭壁林立，惊险无比。突然，谷转，水急，浪花飞溅。因其山形如鸟笼，人们便称其为铁笼山。山上曾是古战场，并有中军帐遗址，昔日"姜维大战铁笼山"就发生在此处，这里也是当年司马昭用泉水救军士之地，至今汩汩泉水终年不断，已出土司马印、戟、戈、箭头等多种文物。

7. 洮坪原始森林游览区

洮坪原始森林游览区位于礼县西南的上坪乡，它是一片原始森林，生活着各种野生动物，植物种类也特别繁多，木本植物就有 300 余种。稀有动物有林麝、马麝、青羊、红腹锦鸡、云豹、毛冠鹿、羚羊、熊等 50 余种。茫茫林海，盛产各种野生药材，如大黄、黄芪、柴胡、当归等。进入林区，山大沟深，壁峻岩秀，形若麦积，状若馒头，又似石板竖立，奇特而险峻。水流清清，穿林越石，瀑布丛生，一派安静宜人的景象。森林深处有一大沟，沟内溪流纵横，曲径通幽，时而可见一股股的溪水从山顶跌落而下，沿沟层峦叠嶂，怪石林立，遍地奇花异草，满山杂树茂密。沿沟行走，景色转换，变幻无穷，万种风情令人目不暇接。大宝山、宝瓶口、双塔崖等景点让游客终生难忘。

8. 大河边草原风情游览区

大河边草原位于礼县县城西南 75 千米处的上坪乡境内，草原面积达 20 万亩。这里水草丰茂，牛羊成群，生活着数千来自甘南、陇南等地的藏、汉牧民。热情的牧民欢迎来自远方的游客，为游客提供训练有素的马匹和其他所需的物品。游客可以骑着马在草原任意驰骋，领略独特的草原风光，体验牧民生活，回归大自然，感受大自然的美妙。

9. 红河水库度假区

红河水库位于礼县县城东北 40 千米处的红河乡的双石沟。它是一座集灌溉、防洪、养鱼、旅游观光等为一体的中型水库。水库于 1957 年 2 月动工，1959 年 1 月竣工。水库建成后除了发挥其应有的作用外，库区独特的风光吸引了大批的游客。每逢周末或假期，游客们在此划船赏景，游泳钓鱼，使平静的水库呈现出一派热闹非凡的场面。

10. 翠峰观生态风景区

翠峰观位于礼县县城东南 7.5 千米处，是礼县古八景之一——翠峰松涛所在地。其山势俊秀、高耸入云，苍松翠柏，芳草争艳，重峦叠嶂，庙宇、楼阁凌空筑就，让人觉得神秘而幽静。道观建筑年代无考，翠峰松涛却令人难忘，当微风清清吹过，绿波荡漾，松涛之声在山谷中回荡，恰似大海波涛又似万马奔腾。后人只能见到院中有半块残碑，因磨损严重，字迹不清，洒水侧视之，有"（南朝）天启元年，辛酉，闰二月二十日""浙人松屏詹里"下有"进士第巡陕西……乙卯秋八月"等字，可知詹里历经六年的艰辛，"翠峰观"才最终得以建成。

1958 年，因大炼钢铁运动，百年的参天古树遭砍伐，庙宇、殿堂被毁坏。近年来，人们植树造林，仿古创新重修庙宇，庙宇又重现于悬崖峭壁之上，上接蓝天，下临深谷，树遮花掩，犹如仙境，是旅游避暑的风水宝地。

11. 黄金寺

黄金寺位于永兴乡友好村，"礼县佛教协会"就设在这里。黄金寺建于何朝何代已无从考证，但相传古代该寺僧众颇多，规模宏大，寺庙建筑约在明朝被毁坏。后世在耕作过程中，发现了碎砖破瓦及庙宇柱石。于是当地念佛居士募化集资，投工献料，在原址重建此寺；1989 年，礼县佛教协会迁于此处。现该寺占地面积达 3 000 多平方米，有佛殿 2 座，护法殿和山门各 1 座，僧舍 24 间。有各类僧人 16 名，佛教居士 40 余人，常年生活在这里。寺内组织机构健全，僧人们除了诵经、拜佛及其他法事活动外，还从事生产劳动，宣传党的民族宗教政策，为宗教活动的正常开展和民族团结、社会稳定做出了巨大的贡献。

12. 太平山公园

太平山公园位于盐官镇北 1 千米处的太平山，是一处道教活动点，也是休闲游乐的好去处。道观布局合理，院内绿树成荫，"槐抱柏"为此园独特一景。每逢农历初一、十五日，天水、西和、礼县等地的善男信女都来此朝拜，场面宏大，气势非凡。

13. 苗河水库度假区

苗河水库位于礼县县城北 30 千米处的罗坝乡的苗河村，是深受人们喜爱的休闲、娱乐的好去处。这里空气清新，环境幽静，吸引了许多游客。它虽然只是一座小型水库，但集防洪、灌溉、发电、养殖于一体，已被开发为旅游观光之地。水库于 1974 年 4 月动工修建，1976 年 9 月竣工，总容量 800 万立方米，可供养殖水面 500 亩，年捕鱼 2 000 千克以上，水库装机容量 500 千瓦。库区整体建筑错落有致。库区水面形成九道湾，在水面划船，犹如泛舟长江三峡，山清水秀，峰峦叠嶂，苍松翠柏与各种经济林木漫山遍野，竞相辉映。

14. 赵世延家庙碑

赵世延家庙碑位于礼县县城南 1 千米处的赵世延家庙遗址。元仁宗延祐三年（1316）秋建。由龙首、碑身、龟跌等三部分组成，碑高 3.5

米，宽 1.3 米，厚 0.24 米。为翰林学士程钜夫撰文，大书法家赵孟頫书丹并篆额。面额书"敕赐赵世延家庙碑"八个字，正面四周阴刻串枝莲文，中间刻文皆为楷书，从右数起，竖刻 33 行，每行 64 字，共 1 230 余字。碑文记载了翰林学士承旨、中书平章政事赵世延祖孙三代六英为建立和巩固元朝政权所创的丰功伟绩。赵世延先祖为雍古族人，故又称"雍古氏家庙碑"，该碑对研究元朝历史及书法艺术有极高价值。

15. 文　庙

文庙大殿位于礼县县城东大街的礼县宾馆院内。据《秦州新志》记载："文庙始建于明万历三十八年（1610），初建城东锦屏山麓，后迁县南之西关，顺治十三年（1656）署县事欧阳缄改迁此地，康熙年间、乾隆四年（1739）、道光十九年（1839）先后重修。"以大殿为中心，有棂星门、魁星阁、乡贤祠和名宦祠等群体建筑，规模宏大，共计三院，40 余间。1958 年被改为政府招待所，部分被拆除改为新型建筑。现存大殿一座，面阔五间，长 22 米，进深四间，宽 17 米，重檐歇山顶，保存完好，现在为县级文物保护单位。

16. 赤土山园林

赤土山园林位于礼县县城东 2 千米处，因山体呈红色，而得其名。《礼县志》曰："县东四里赤土山有一石上足迹长五尺，传为陨石。"故得"赤土显迹"之名，为礼县古八景之一。1996 年，县委、县政府对赤土山园林进行了规划修建，实施田、水、林、路综合治理。如今，古建筑与新建筑交相辉映，古柏与新植的稀有树种连成一片。每年的农历三月二十八日到四月八日，赤土山园林举行盛大的庙会，诵经唱戏，善男信女纷纷来此进香，小商贩们在道路两旁竞相叫卖，游人们赶来看戏游玩，盛况空前，非常热闹。随着礼县旅游事业的快速发展，越来越多的游客来这里休闲、娱乐、观光。

17. 王仁裕神道碑

王仁裕神道碑位于县城南 10 千米处的石桥乡斩龙湾村，全称"周故太子少师王公神道碑"，又有王仁裕墓及墓志铭，是一座全面记述五代著名政治家、文学家王仁裕的墓葬碑。北宋宰相王仁裕的门生李昉撰文，张贺书丹并篆额，王仁裕嫡孙王永锡于宋朝雍熙元年（984）立碑。

18. 新中川烈士陵园

历史悠久的礼县，自古为兵家必争之地。三国时蜀汉丞相诸葛亮两次亲临祁山讨伐曹魏，建立了不朽的功勋。红军在长征途中，红二方面军兵分三路，途经礼县，左路——红六军，由军长陈伯钧、政委王震及参谋长彭绍辉率领，经宕昌过闾井、马坞，抵达礼县县城。后经崖城等四乡，在红河集中，就地扩军筹资，最后离开礼县南下徽县、两当。中路军——二方面军指挥部，二军四师、三十二军，从岷县、理川出发，经闾井，到达礼县上坪，后经洮坪、江口、龙林去西和、成县方向，与敌军鲁大昌部遭遇，俘敌 30 多人，缴获 30 支枪、20 匹马。右路军——二军六师，由师长贺炳炎、政委廖汉生率领，由宕昌出发，经礼县的铨水、白河等六乡，去西和的太石河方向，借以迷惑敌人。红二方面军在礼县境内共活动 16 天，足迹遍布 20 多个乡（镇），所到之处向人民群众宣传革命真理，撒播革命火种。

随着解放战争的第一枪打响，解放大军以锐不可当之势，迅速解放了全国大部分省区。解放前夕，国民党在礼县的最后一任县长阎广，曾在盐官、祁山等地修筑城堡、钻山成洞，妄图与敌——九军响应，进行负隅顽抗。一一九军二二四师的一个营驻扎在盐官城内，四门把守，昼夜放哨。1949 年 8 月初，天水解放，第一野战军第七军二十师五十八团副团长王鼎新带领解放军进逼礼县，在充分了解敌情的前提下，解放军凭借秋季玉米田的掩护，连夜赶赴盐官城外。第一营士兵从上磨（新中川）草滩一带，绕道王城，守住西门；第二、三营士兵由苏家城到马坪山一带主攻东南门。深夜发起总攻击，在劝告和登云梯攻城没有成功的情况下，解放军以少数兵力佯装攻东门，重兵调集猛攻南门，敌人果然中计，南门攻开。经过激战，敌军投降。敌营长崔学礼被擒。整个战斗中，解放军有 7 名指战员牺牲（副连长 1 人，排长 1 人，战士 5 人），还有一名群众在护送伤员中牺牲。战斗结束后，军长彭绍辉、政委冼恒汉在小天水召开庆功会，表彰了有功人员，并将 8 名英勇牺牲的烈士安葬在新中川，将其开辟为陵园。为了褒扬革命烈士精神，中共礼县委员会、礼县人民政府于 1996 年 10 月在陵园树碑一座，拓宽了陵园，新建了围墙和门，并将其列为当地重要的爱国主义教育基地。

19. 高寺头遗址

高寺头遗址位于石桥乡高寺头村，面积 6 000 平方米，文化层厚处达 4 米，历年有石、陶、骨器出土，地面遗有大量夹沙、泥质、细泥质的灰，以及褐、红、黄色陶片，有钵、盆、罐、瓶、鬲等器形，出土的典型器物有"人首形器盖"，是史前人像造型的代表之一，艺术价值很高。该遗址属仰韶、齐家、周代等多种文化类型的遗址。1947 年裴文中首次发现，1960 年《考古学报》第 2 期有报道，1983 年《考古》第 12 期有纪要，1986 年省文物考古研究所进行小面积试掘。属省级文物保护单位。

20. 石碑下遗址

石碑下遗址位于城关镇石碑村北，面积约 30 000 平方米。文化层厚 0.5～2 米。1947 年裴文中首先发现石、陶、青铜器多件。20 世纪 70 年代出土细泥质红陶钵，双耳、三耳红陶罐和砍砸石器等。属仰韶、齐家文化遗址。

21. 瑶峪墓群

瑶峪墓群位于石桥乡瑶峪村，分布在长 1 千米，宽 0.5 千米的平地上。

地埂截面暴露残墓数座，有砖、土墓两种，坐北向南，顶拱形，墓口在2~2.5米见方之间，离地表2米以上。当地农民在修梯田、取土中发现遗物较多，陶器有盆、罐、盘、簋、鼎、屋、井、灶等，铜器有马啣、带勾矛、镞、镜、五铢钱等。从出土文物可判断其为汉代墓群。

22. 城隍庙

城隍庙位于礼县城隍庙街，始建年代无考。据现有资料证实，该庙于明朝万历四十六年（1618）重修，清代多次维修，民国中期扩建，占地面积约2 000平方米，庙宇坐北朝南，中轴线上有仪门、戏楼、卷棚、正殿、后堂、一进四院，东西对称，有钟鼓楼、廊房、厢房数十间，主要建筑有三殿三楼，共十四间，面积在45~63平方米之间。多系硬顶木构建筑。1987年，主体部分进行维修。该庙是古代寺院建筑的代表。

23. 红军墓

红军墓位于草坪乡龙池村东山上。1936年10月7日，中国工农红军二方面军六军团过境礼县，从罗家堡去红河的路途中突遇敌军包围和空袭，军直模范师冲出，十六师政委晏福生负重伤，卫生队后勤人员投入战斗，一百多人牺牲。在龙池村山下面有数十名战士牺牲，就地埋葬，现有合葬墓两处。

思考与实践

1. 礼县大堡子山秦公墓为何有如此大的影响？它见证了历史上的哪些人和事？
2. 我们应该怎样继承和发扬"诸葛亮的精神"？
3. 参观祁山诸葛亮庙，了解诸葛亮六出祁山的经过。
4. "盐井祠"仅仅是为了供奉"盐神"而修建的吗？

5. 人们为何要修造庙宇殿堂？你认为它们的价值在哪里？

6. 试分析名胜古迹和自然生态旅游各有哪些优点。

7. 你对这些旅游景点的总的印象如何？礼县旅游资源开发需要注意什么？

8. 古遗址对我们的启示是什么？

9. 书法史上的"四体"各指什么？"赵体"的特点是什么？请到"赵世延家庙碑"去观摩。

10. 建造水库的最初目的不是为了旅游观光，为何后来都被开发为旅游景点，你受到了什么启发？

11. 利用节假日参观各旅游景点，并写出观后感。

12. 你认为还有哪些地方可以列为旅游景点，作为热爱大自然、热爱祖国的教育基地，请调查并写出报告。

13. 请你构想礼县旅游事业发展的蓝图，并预测前景和收益。

第三章 地方工农业产品

1. 苹果

礼县是著名的优质苹果产地，多种苹果闻名全国。"红元帅""红星""红冠"苹果最为著名。特别是 1963 年与天水市花牛村同期出口的礼县"三红"苹果，以"花牛"为牌子，成功打入了国际市场。礼县早被列为"花牛"苹果外销生产基地。

"三红"苹果的主要特点是结果早、产量高、果型端正、果顶五棱明显；充分成熟后为深红色或艳红色；果面蜡质较厚，果肉淡黄，酥脆汁多，有芳香味，酸甜适度，耐贮藏。有的单果重达 300 克，堪与美国王牌苹果蛇果媲美。据测定，"三红"苹果含糖12%以上，含有多种维生素、矿物质和增强人脑记忆力的微量元素，曾荣获国家农产品优质奖。

2. 八盘梨

八盘梨是甘肃特产，也是礼县优良梨种之一。因其形状扁圆如盘，所以被称为"八盘梨"。农历八月成熟，且可收藏到冬季食用。其特点是果实大，肉质细脆嫩白，果汁多，略有酸味，耐贮藏，含糖量高于一般的梨。它不仅味道鲜美，而且具有一定的药用价值，具有润肺、止咳、化痰等功效，本地人喜欢把八盘梨用冰糖煮蒸后再吃。

据有关资料记载：礼县八盘梨早在明朝嘉靖年间就开始大量栽培。20 世纪 60 年代初，八盘梨的种植面积和产量达到历史最高水平。产区主要分布在西汉水上游一带。另据传说，八盘梨曾是朝廷的贡品。1996 年，在全省果树技术会议上，礼县被定为八盘梨生产基地。

3. 大　蒜

紫皮或白皮大蒜都是礼县著名产品。特点是个大、瓣肥、叶多、味辣，实为调味之佳品，杀菌之能手。蒜薹更是色泽明亮，味美纯正，营养成分高。

4. 柿　子

礼县柿子产地分布在龙林、雷坝、王坝一带，年产10多万千克，主要品种是"四棱柿""社降黄""君迁之"等。成熟前的"青柿果"，人们既可以利用桑叶或生石灰、微火温水加工成脆甜可口的"酱柿"，亦可加工成"柿饼"，还可以制成"酒柿子"。酒柿子是礼县又一地方特产，用白酒把柿子浸蘸后装坛，或用高粱酒醅与柿子混合装坛，密封数月后启封食用，酒柿子皮肉黄色或棕色，酒味浓郁醇正，味美甘甜，色味俱佳，为馈赠亲友之珍品。副产品柿霜、柿蒂、根、皮等能入药，青柿果榨汁为柿油，能代替油漆染漆雨伞、渔网。

5. 石　榴

礼县石榴主要有"白仁石榴"和"红仁石榴"两种。白仁石榴，皮白色，粒大，汁液多，味甜，品质中上。红仁石榴，成熟后，皮色艳红，汁多味甜，品质上乘。石榴的根、枝、皮可以做驱除蛔虫的药物。果皮性湿，味酸涩，主治久泻久痢、脱肛等症。礼县石榴产地主要分布在雷坝乡坪头村、鱼池村，肖良乡的桃林等地。

6. 花　椒

花椒是礼县的著名农产品之一，也是当地人民的主要经济来源。礼县花椒的栽培历史久，技术高。许多品种都能在这里生长、开花、结果。如每年6月份采摘的"油椒"和"大红袍"；7月成熟的"七月椒"和"羊毛椒"；8月收获的"八月椒"和"迟绵椒"等。

花椒属于芸香科灌木或小乔木，茎秆棕褐色，多分枝，枝上有刺，嫩枝被短柔毛。叶子椭圆形，表面深绿色，背面淡绿色。果实球形，紫红色，密生有疣状突起的腺点。种子也呈球形，黑色，有光泽。当果实成熟时自然裂开，种子暴露在外。果皮的基部仍然相连，像切开的皮球，直径为 0.1～0.5 厘米，外果皮表面极粗糙，颜色从红紫色到红棕色，具有许多疣状突起的油腺；内果皮光滑，呈淡黄色。晒干后，无论是原状使用还是加工成粉末，都是上等的调味品。

一般而言，花椒的质量与它的成熟时间有关，成熟早的质量好，但树龄较短，一般结果 7～12 年，"迟绵椒"质量较差，且树龄较长，一般结果 40～50 年。"油椒"和"大红袍"是礼县花椒中的优良品种，成熟早，果实色香浓郁。"大红袍"果实较大，结果较稀，果皮颜色艳红，晒干除籽后，外果皮呈红色，内果皮呈淡黄色。"油椒"果实大，果皮为深红色，油脂丰富，味浓而香，不刺鼻，质量优于"大红袍"，是礼县花椒中的佼佼者。礼县花椒畅销国内，远销日本、罗马尼亚和东南亚各国。

花椒的秆、枝、叶、果实都有特殊的用途。果实的外皮既是香料，又是中药材，可暖胃除风，消食解胀，治疗吐泻痢疾。种子既可种植，又可以制造"花椒油"或"花椒液"，它们都是油辣、麻酥的调味品，具有特殊的强烈香气，味麻辣而持久。油渣可做饲料或肥料。叶子可以食用，也可防虫、入药。花椒耐干旱，对土壤的要求不严格，适应性极强，县内大部分地方都有出产，西汉水下游的江口、龙林、雷坝等地的产品最佳。

7. 烟 叶

生长于礼县县城周围的烟叶，质地优良，无农药污染。晒干后，颜色金黄，烟味平顺，吸用可口，有香味，不刺鼻，不呛口。具有防虫驱蚊、清爽提神之功效。

烟叶属于茄科，是一年生草本植物，性喜温暖，耐干旱。礼县主要生产烤烟和晒烟两种。晒烟不做深加工，经日光晒干便可直接吸用。尤其以石桥圣泉所产的烟叶最为著名。

8. 王坝豆腐

用黑黄豆或黄豆精制的豆腐在礼县很受欢迎。制作过程极其精细和复杂：先将黄豆磨成小颗粒，除去皮在冷水中浸泡软，再用手推小磨磨成黏稠状的浆。用沸水融化这种浆，再用纱布过滤。纱布内为豆渣。过滤后的浆进行蒸煮，煮到一定的火候，把当地产的土盐加入锅中，一团团的豆花便会浮出来。把豆花捞入豆腐箱，放凉后豆腐就做成了。豆腐的食用方法甚多，既可凉拌，又可炒可烩、可炸可煮。无论用什么方法烹饪豆腐，都味道鲜美，营养丰富，含热量高，且含有多种维生素和氨基酸，具有细嫩清香的口味，深受男女老幼的喜爱。

9. 松花蜜

礼县松花蜜为蜜蜂在蜂房中酿成的糖类物质的精制品，是半透明的、黏稠的、半流动的液体，经过加热，呈琥珀色。若用木棒挑起则蜂蜜向下流，连续不断而成折叠状，夏季如食油状，有光泽；冬季则结晶，状如蜡油，并含有颗粒状物。气味芳香，味极甜。具有润肺补中、滑肠止痛、解毒等功效。

10. 核桃麦芽糖

先将小麦发芽，晒干，捣碎，再将磨碎的玉米粒在锅中蒸煮，加入麦芽粉后，过滤去渣，再用人火煮到黏稠状，加入核桃仁，出锅放凉即成。核桃麦芽糖呈半透明的红棕色固体。遇热它就变软，放冷它会变硬。

由于核桃含有丰富的脂肪和蛋白质，具有健脑、益肾、增加头发光泽的功效；麦芽、玉米又含有糖分和各种维生素。所以，核桃麦芽糖黏度极强，食之香甜适宜，营养丰富，颇受礼县人民的喜爱。

11. 核 桃

核桃是礼县重要的经济树种之一，种植历史悠久，有露仁核桃、大麻核桃、薄皮核桃、油核桃等。以薄皮核桃为多，外皮薄而易剥，肉厚味香，具有含油量高、出仁率高、蛋白质含量高等特点，是很好的滋补品。核桃既可食用，又可榨油，长期食用具有健肾、补智、乌发的作用。主要分布在燕河、太塘、中坝、白河、桥头、王坝、滩坪等地，年产量约18万千克。

12. 青铜器仿制品

礼县出土的一批青铜器年代久远、造型精美，震惊了世界。当地人民设计和制造了各种仿制品，形状、颜色均与真品相似。其品质高雅，色彩美丽，而且易于保存，物美价廉，是值得收藏的艺术品，也是上等的礼品和纪念品。

13. 地方酒

（1）秦皇御酒。

秦皇御酒是礼县秦皇酒厂生产的佳酿，具有清澈透明、醇香浓厚、绵甜甘爽、回味无穷等特点。

（2）酩淋酒。

酩淋酒历史悠久，风味独特，在礼县境内颇受欢迎。它以小麦和玉米为主要原料酿制而成，酒色浊而白。加热后饮用，甘甜而清淡，味醇香而沉，清爽而提神，具有生津解渴、醉不口干等特点，经常被用作中药引子，誉满礼县。酪淋酒主要出产在草坪、滩坪等地。

> **思考与实践**

1. 花牛苹果指什么？为何得此名？特点是什么？
2. 礼县"三红"苹果主要产地是哪里，为什么？
3. 花椒有哪些主要品种？花椒的成熟时间与花椒品质有关吗？
4. 柿子的加工方法有几种？酒柿、柿饼、浆柿各有什么特点？
5. 礼县的农产品有何特点？原产品著名还是加工产品著名？
6. 你认为应该如何提高礼县农产品的附加值？
7. 王坝豆腐、核桃麦芽糖的加工过程说明了什么？
8. 你还知道哪些特色农产品？请简单介绍。
9. 你认为旅游事业与农产品有关系吗？若有，关系如何？你还知道哪些特色农产品，请介绍它们的生长环境、栽培技术、经济效益。
10. 极少的地方工业说明了什么？
11. 酪淋酒深受人们喜爱，何以发展缓慢？
12. 你还知道礼县民间有哪些手工制作？请描述。

第四章 山野菜

1. 羊肚菌

羊肚菌,别名羊肚菜,因形似倒翻过来的羊肚子而得名。羊肚菌种类繁多,有黑脉羊肚菌、粗腿羊肚菌、尖顶羊肚菌、小羊肚菌、高羊肚菌、褐赤羊肚菌、美味羊肚菌等数种。羊肚菌有很高的食用价值,用羊肚菌制作的菜肴,营养丰富,香气宜人,有独特的口感风味。羊肚菌还具有促进人体生长发育、促进造血、增进免疫力等功能,是强身健脑、美容、提高智力的天然保健食品。每千克价值 1 000 美元左右。主要产于山峪、王坝、草坪、桥头、沙金、洮坪、罗坝、湫山等地。

2. 蕨 菜

蕨菜,形似手指,又称"佛手",俗称"吉祥菜"。礼县生长的蕨菜具有组织细软、色泽绿、味醇、质粘、鲜嫩等特点。它系野生草本植物,生长在荒山野岭,未受污染,含有多种营养成分,具有特殊的营养价值。全株可作药用,性寒味甘,有清热止痛的作用。

我国人民食用蕨菜有很长的历史,最初它是普通人家饭桌上的一般的山野菜,后来进入达官贵人的食谱,据说甚至成了皇帝的贡品,可见其美味非同一般。

每年春季,蕨菜的幼叶柄鲜嫩味美。既可当季食用,又可晒制干菜,或盐渍加工。就晒制干菜而言,要经过一道复杂的工序,即先把采摘到的鲜蕨菜在沸水中焯一下,然后阴干,截成三寸左右的小段,捆绑好后晒干。有时还要喷洒少许叶绿素,使其色泽鲜艳诱人,水煮后凉拌,色香味俱佳,畅销国内外市场。

3. 苦芥菜

礼县的西南山区的小麦、黑麦田地里或山坡上盛产苦芥菜,这是礼县的又一风味特产。苦芥菜属于十字花科,是一种当年生草本植物,茎秆直,独立,叶深绿色,开白色小花,果实黑色。幼嫩茎叶含钙、维生素 B 等,鲜菜焯后即可食用,用植物油、辣椒、盐和其他辅料,味道独特,略带苦味。若把苦芥菜切成小段加细盐揉搓均匀,装入坛子,密封,数月后便可食用。经过盐渍的苦芥菜易于保存,食用时启封,颜色变为金黄,可以用植物油及其他辅料搅拌,风味独特,脆嫩爽口,苦味全无,咸中带香,是当地人们喜爱的一种野菜,也是地方宴席中的上等菜肴。经常食用苦芥菜,能解毒利尿,防治疾病。

4. 木龙头

木龙头也是受当地人喜欢的一种野菜。木龙头又叫乌龙头,属于五加科,是木龙头树的幼芽,是礼县山林地区所产的食药两用的名贵野菜。木龙头树每年春天长出的紫红色"弹头状"幼芽,状若灯笼,酷似拇指,生长较长时,其自然抽穗成为树叶。它含有钙、维生素 B 等,入口清脆,微苦,热量低,是理想的减肥野生名菜,药效明显,有健胃利便,活血止痛的功效。木龙头菜既可新鲜食用,又可晒为干菜,还可以腌制成咸菜或醋菜。鲜食时,将其在沸水中焯后,再在凉水中冷却,挤干残余的水,泼上热植物油,加上蒜泥和其他调味品。木龙头菜香脆可口、清爽宜人、略带药味,吃后令人回味无穷。

思考与实践

1. 本章提到的几种山野菜你认识吗?春季是它们最好的采集时节,请观察它们的生长。
2. 羊肚菌营养丰富,价格不菲,产地较多,为何没有广泛栽培?
3. 蕨菜的食用方法有哪些?

4. 苦芥菜的营养价值是什么？

5. 木龙头的药理作用是什么？

6. 这几种山野菜你都品尝过吗，感觉怎样？

7. 试了解有多少山野菜已经被人们广泛种植，前景如何？收益如何？

8. 你认为礼县山野菜资源得到充分利用了吗？如果没有，应该如何发展这一产业？

9. 你还知道哪些山野菜？试了解它们的生长情况、营养价值、食用方法。

第五章 中药材

1. 大 黄

大黄是礼县的拳头产品。大黄为"掌叶大黄",又叫"黄良""将军",是一种多年生草本植物。喜好阳光充足,土质结构疏松、透水性好的黑色土壤。据有关史料记载,礼县种植大黄已有数百年的历史,其主要产于西南部的铨水一带,所以,礼县大黄又称"铨黄"。铨水大黄的出口一直占我国大黄出口的50%,为全国之首。从20世纪50年代开始出口,产品销往东南亚及西欧等地区,被称为"中国铨黄",1971年注册为"双鹿牌"商标。1981年,意大利米兰左卡公司来礼县拍摄了大黄广告片,1983年,西德费尔摩根公司来礼县进行大黄生产的实地考察,1984年,在全国出口商品基地、专厂建设成果质量鉴定会议上,"双鹿牌"大黄荣获中华人民共和国对外经济贸易部《出口商品荣誉证书》。

掌叶大黄为蓼科高大草本植物,根粗壮,茎直立、中心空,表面光滑无毛,根生叶大,有长柄;叶片宽心形或近圆形,正面光滑无毛,背面被白色毛,茎生叶较小,生长多数紫红色或黄白色小花,果实棕色呈三角形。大黄是中药中的一味主要泻药,味苦且寒,具有涤肠、荡胃之功效。

将大黄种子培育成大黄苗,然后间苗移栽,无须施肥,其幼苗就能苗壮成长。大黄一般在8、9月份采挖,肥厚多汁的块茎可煮吃,也可像水果一样食用。大黄块茎要切成三段,上段称为"苏吉子",下段称为"水根子",中段称为"大黄"。"大黄"为上等。大黄挖出后要立即熏干,否则就会发霉,而且熏烤的时间越久越好。

干大黄形状不一,有近圆柱形、长圆锥形等。刮去粗皮的大黄呈棕黄色或红棕色,可见类白色网纹或菊花形星点。未刮去外皮的呈褐色,表面有疙瘩状隆起,有横纹或纵皱纹。截面多凹凸不平,质地坚实,中心较松软，呈橙红色或红棕色，稍有油性，气味清香特殊，味苦微涩。

2. 黄 芪

黄芪为豆科多年生草本植物，主根深长，棒状，稍带木质，不易折断，外皮呈红色或棕黄色，茎直立，上部多分枝，光滑或略被柔毛，种子黑色，肾形。成品黄芪为圆柱形，上粗下细，表面呈灰黄色或淡褐色，全体有不整齐的纵纹或纵沟，质地坚硬，略有韧性和粉性。断面纤维性极强，外层是黄白色较疏松，中间有黄色的菊花心。味甜微臭，并有豆腥气。具有补气固表，利水退肿，托疮排脓之药理作用。黄芪主要产于礼县西北和西南的部分乡村，年产量19万千克以上。

3. 柴 胡

柴胡的植物学描述为：多年生草本植物，根直立少分支。茎秆坚硬直立，并作"之"字形弯曲，叶子表面绿色，背面淡绿色。开黄色五瓣小花。果实椭圆形。干燥的柴胡根呈圆锥形，主根顺直坚韧，外皮灰褐色。断面呈木质纤维性，黄白色，味微苦辛，略有香气。柴胡有退热、疏肝，升举阳气之功。

4. 甘 草

野生甘草为多年生草本植物，根茎圆柱形，主根长而大，外皮红褐色。茎秆直立，稍带木质，被有白色短毛或腺磷。叶片卵形具有长柄。开紫红色花。果实镰刀状或弯曲成环状，密被褐色的刺状腺毛。黑色的种子呈圆形。药用甘草呈圆柱形，红褐色有明显的纵横沟纹。切面中央稍下陷，质地坚实而重，断面具有纤维性和粉性，且有明显的环纹和菊花心。微具特异的香气，味甜，具有补脾益气、清热解毒、润肺止渴、调和诸药的功效。

5. 当归

当归是多年生草本植物，主根粗壮，呈不规则圆柱形。外皮褐色。根头略膨大，支根数条至十余条。茎秆直立，紫色，有明显的纵纹，光滑无毛。开白色花，果实椭圆形，成熟后从合生面分开，淡紫色。根分为三部分，根头俗称"归头"，主根俗称"归身"，支根及根尾部俗称"归尾"。外皮灰棕色，全身有纵纹。"归头"上端圆平，有茎叶的残基，常有环状皱纹；"归身"略呈圆柱形，凸凹不平，生有许多支根；"归尾"上粗下细，多扭曲，有疙瘩的须根痕迹。质地柔韧，断面黄白色有裂隙。中间有浅棕色环纹，并有多数棕色油点。气清香浓厚而特异，味甘微苦辛。礼县出产的当归虽然没有岷县出产的当归有名，但其质优价廉，具有补血和养血、调经止痛、去淤生新等多种功能，实为妇科不可缺少的良药。当归是礼县经济作物的骨干产品。主要产于湫山、罗坝、洮坪、白关、沙金、草坪等地。

6. 党参

党参是礼县大宗药材产品之一，分野生和家种的两种，多年生野生党参的功效超过"白糖参"，其外皮粗糙，头部硕大的叫"狮子头"，截面似菊花的叫"菊花心"。礼县既有家种党参，又有从文县引进的"纹当"和从临洮引进的"白条党"。野生党参分布在礼县西南部分乡村，人工栽培的党参主要出产在洮坪、白关等地。

思考与实践

1. 大黄有哪些药理作用？
2. "人参无过，大黄无功"是说大黄没有作用吗？

3. 礼县大黄何以驰名世界？
4. 找一些干大黄，观察其外形特点，了解其种植技巧。
5. 黄芪的特点是什么？
6. 甘草何以有"调和诸药"的作用？请做调查。
7. 当归的"三部分"与大黄的"三部分"是否一样？
8. 礼县还有哪些主要的野生或家种中药材，请了解，并分析其前景。

第六章 地方小吃

饮食文化是中华文明中不可分割的一部分。礼县的小吃，虽然不及南方各地丰富，但因其特殊的地理位置和文化传统，无论是本地发明的小吃、零食，还是从外界传入的小吃、零食，都具有自己独特的风味。

1. 热面皮

将面粉和成团，用水洗出面筋，再放入白铁皮或铝质的特制薄形蒸锣中蒸成片。食用时，趁热切成条状，再加上几块蒸熟的面筋，加上辣椒油、蒜泥、醋和其他辅料。热面皮具有味浓而不腻、久吃不厌、回味无穷等特点，深受人们的喜爱。热面皮若冷却后再食用，则晶莹透明，兼具面条的柔韧和凉粉的滑爽。

2. 猪油饼

猪油饼，是礼县颇有地方特色的风味小吃。猪油饼以温热猪油、植物油、小麦面粉、生姜、花椒、葱花、食盐等为原料，将黏稠状的"油面"与发酵好的"起面"按1∶3的比例充分糅合制成圆形饼，放在两面可加热的锅中，烤熟。其颜色金黄，吃起来酥而不散，油而不腻，清香酥脆，口味极佳，香气飘溢，久吃不厌。猪油饼和面技艺要求很高，大多数当地人都善于此技艺。有时用鸡蛋作馅，制作成馅饼，称为"鸡蛋猪油饼"。在礼县城区，猪油饼可以称得上是人见人爱的早餐食品。

3. 饸饹面

饸饹面也是礼县当地的风味小吃之一,其制作方法古朴、独特。先把荞麦磨成粉末,然后再做成饸饹面,既可凉调冷吃,又可配以各种臊子汤,味道鲜美,是礼县人民尤其是妇女们最喜爱的夏季小吃之一。

4. 臊子面

面食是礼县人的主食,多年来,人们发明了很多面食加工方法,臊子面就是其中之一。臊子面既可以机器制作,又可以手工制作。就手工臊子面而言,面要擀得轻薄如纸,切面讲究手法,宽的形如葱叶,细的形如绳线。拌汤则可荤可素、可辣可酸,原料都是本地特产,配料新鲜,色、香、味独特。要是再上用鲜肉和各种山珍做的臊子,一碗令人垂涎欲滴的礼县臊子面就出锅了。

5. 肉夹馍

先把鲜猪肉在卤水中炖好,加上用蜂蜜熬的汁和其他辅料,并保持一定的温度。食用时,把肉切成碎片,再将准备好的馍切开,将碎肉片放入,再浸洒上一些肉汤。如果急需享用,伸手抓起来即可。礼县肉夹馍汤香味浓,肉鲜嫩而不油腻,馍酥脆而清香,是深受当地人喜爱的早餐食品。

6. 酒 醅

酒醅,又叫醪糟,是一种极好的夏季小吃。把用酒曲发酵好的小麦放在一个大盆子里。食用时,依据个人口味,加少许凉开水和砂糖。礼县酒醅的特点是甘甜并有酒味,小麦粒松软可口,具有清爽提神,消暑解渴的作用。

7. 宽川凉粉

  冷凉粉在礼县县城常有出售。它是用荞麦精制而成的，先把荞麦磨成小颗粒，除去荞麦皮，和成面团，再经过揉搓后过滤，做成面浆，用文火对面浆加热、搅拌直到煮熟，盛入盆子或其他容器，冷却成型。食用时，将其切成小方块盛在一大碗中，配以植物油、花椒油、蒜泥、醋和其他调味品，便成了四季皆宜的小吃。

8. 烧 烤

  在礼县县城，一到晚上，沿街多是出售烧烤的摊点。烤羊肉串、烤鱼、烤鸡肉、烤土豆等都可以在商贩处品尝。礼县烧烤具有其独特的口味，脆酥爽口，鲜嫩宜人，吸引过路人来品尝。比如，烤羊肉串——羊肉置在炭火上熏烤，用花椒、辣椒、胡椒、盐等做辅料，食之香脆而不油腻，肉鲜嫩而无膻味。

9. 盐官扁食

  盐官扁食是礼县当地的一种风味小吃，它是将和好的小麦面粉，通过手工或机器制成薄片，再切成梯形小方块，放上拌好的馅儿，用手捏成鱼状，在沸水中煮熟。扁食的馅儿种类较多，可荤可素，有韭菜鸡蛋、白葱豆腐、韭菜土豆，还可以是精肉或羊肉等。煮熟的扁食还可以配上各种臊子汤，其特点是：馅嫩面柔，口感极好，久吃不厌。

10. 永兴扯面

永兴扯面的做法是在小麦面粉中加入适量的灰粉或食盐制成面团，然后将面团分为一寸左右的面段，表面再涂上植物油，防止相互粘连、变硬。制作时，用小擀面杖擀开，两端用手抓住扯开，经过几次对折和拉开，再投入沸水中煮熟。食用时，依据个人口味配上不同的臊子汤，就可以享用了。扯面滑爽可口，柔韧晶亮，深受人们的喜爱。

思考与实践

1. 礼县小吃有哪些主要特点？
2. 礼县小吃的原料有什么特点？
3. 小吃的特点说明礼县经济发展水平如何？
4. 你知道礼县还有哪些特色小吃？请描述它们的原料、制作过程及特点。
5. 品尝礼县的特色小吃，并说出它们的特点。
6. 自己尝试做一下礼县的特色小吃。

第七章 补充资料

1. 珍奇鱼种——娃娃鱼

娃娃鱼是一种稀有的珍贵鱼种，礼县西南部的山林小溪盛产。其特点是无鱼鳞，身体侧扁，背灰色，鱼腹为淡白色。体形似人，有头、颈，以及生有五个小趾的四肢。具有极高的药用价值，能够生肌长骨，俗称"接骨丹"。

2. 礼县县名考

礼县县名来源于地名。隋唐至宋的长道县治，设立在礼县县城东15千米的李家店（现称甸子上）。元朝长道并入西和州，另在今天的城关镇设置"李店、文州蒙古汉军西番军民之元帅府"。由于府治距历时已久的长道县治相当近，所以叫"李店府"。当朝儒士觉得"李"字不雅，就借用同音字"礼"代替，形成了元朝"李"与"礼"混用的情况，《元史百官志七》写为"李店"即可证明，直到明朝设置县时才正式定为"礼"县。

3. 县 城

礼县县城——城关镇，位于县境中部，西汉水和燕子河交汇的地方，城区中心在东经105°，北纬34°，海拔1 403.8米，东距天水97千米，南到武都250千米，北达省城兰州345千米，为全县的政治、经济、文化及交通中心。

礼县开发甚早，周时为秦人发祥地。秦汉时是西县辖地。南北朝时，分属兰仓、汉阳等县。隋唐宋时期分别为长道、潭水、大潭等县。元朝时期，今天的县城一带建立了军民元帅府。明朝初期设立了守御千户所，是军事、民事合一的地方权力机关。明成化九年（1473），割秦州十九里开始设置礼县，实行军民分治。"所城"的西面扩大，修筑南、北、西三面城墙，筑建县城。县城的东墙为所城的西墙。所城和县城各有南北二门，所城的西门叫穿城门。清朝顺治年间，裁所并县，所县二城并为县城。清朝咸丰、同治、光绪以及民国时期进行整修、加固，增设炮台，修筑内墙。民国十八年（1929）县城初具规模，基本完备。城墙周长三里有余，高三点五丈，有四座角楼，一座哨楼，八座炮台，还有营房。城内有大北街、大南街、小南街等四条主要街道，并配有黉学街、广丰街、曲巷、薛家街、隍庙门街、出祠巷、刘家街、鹿家街、三多街、仓院后街、积厚街、潘家宅、学巷等十三条小巷。

民国三十年（1941），礼县县城开始设置镇，叫作"天嘉镇"，1952年改名为城关镇，1958年为城关公社，1983年恢复为城关镇。经过1990年的扩建和2000年的小城镇建设，今天的县城，楼房林立、街道宽敞、市井繁荣，初步具有现代化城镇的规模。

4. 汉代祭天遗址

受国内外各界关注的"秦人探源"工程将继续进行。甘肃省有关部门正在酝酿实施"陇东南秦早期文化研究项目"。2004年，在历时半年的野外调查中，考古人员发现了大型遗址，现在初步确定是一个规模巨大的汉代祭天遗址。

从2004年3月开始，由甘肃省文物考古研究所、陕西省文物考古研究所、中国国家博物馆、北京大学考古文博学院、西北师范大学考古系5家单位共同成立了早期秦文化研究课题组和联合考察队，在礼县博物馆的大力支持、参与和配合下，实施为期六年的"秦早期都城、陵墓和早期秦文化调查和挖掘"项目。

整个调查从2004年3月28日开始，调查队对西汉水上游干流及其支流——漾水河、红河、燕子河、永坪河流域，东起天水市天水乡，西至礼县江口乡，长约 60 千米的地域进行了全面勘察，调查共发现各类遗址 98 处，与 20 世纪 50 年代相比，新发现的有 70 多处。

5. 礼县古八景

礼县古八景是：
（1）赤土显迹，在赤土山。
（2）神泉古洞（古泉养鱼），在古泉村。
（3）圣泉夜月，在圣泉村。
（4）翠峰松涛，在翠峰观。
（5）鸾亭瑞雾，在水湾村。
（6）天嘉福地，在城关镇。
（7）祁山暮雨，在祁山村。
（8）雷峰夕照，在雷王乡。

明朝房思哲留有十一首专门写礼县古景的诗，它们分别是：天嘉福地、赤土显迹、西江感应、垩土无影、翠峰禅寺、元宵神灯、圣泉夜月、广佛玉像、显工无痕、雷王丹灶、黑峪悬石。

清朝雷文渊诗中记有天嘉仙乐、鸾亭瑞雾、汉水春波、祁山暮雨、圣泉夜月、雷峰夕照、神泉古洞、翠峰松涛等八景，原诗如下：

天嘉仙乐
琳宫曾否住神仙，古石瓶中雅韵传。
漫听哀思来鲁壁，翻疑广乐奏钧天。
高山流水参真契，明月清风净俗缘。
为问几人能管领，审音悟到上乘禅。

鸾亭瑞雾
气氤氲辨不明，岚光雾影共纵横。
溟濛豹隐千重合，缥缈鸾翔五彩萦。
山铀连云增瑞霭，崇朝沛雨济苍生。

弗迷何待南车指,愿步层峰顶上行。

汉水春波
曾记观澜广汉滨,源探嶓冢本清沦。
东风巧织涟漪锦,旭日微烘淡荡春。
溪涧流添分燕尾,崖城波合戚鱼鳞。
愿将水鉴同民鉴,好把西江浣俗尘。

祁山暮雨
祁峰巍峙几千秋,雨势潇潇薄暮稠。
故垒当年朝马走,平林此日晚鸣鸠。
照川霞映残红落,绕汉波添浅白流。
我愧子安滕阁宴,西山帘卷怅勾留。

圣泉夜月
涓涓贴地寒泉涌,皎皎当空皓月悬。
水拘蟾轮光满袖,波涵象纬影连天。
出山诚恐清成浊,对镜几经缺又圆。
御旱我曾殷祈祷,幸分膏泽润农田。

雷峰夕照
一峰特立势垂仪,忆昔雷王炼汞时。
丹灶尚余香冉冉,鸟轮徐度影迟迟。
半山云压斜晖淡,五色霞烘晚照奇。
欲觅勾砂回老景,到头谁挽隙驹驰。

神泉古洞
三千界里共飘蓬,灵境谁探峻岭中。
泉隙四通横燕处,洞天一线辟鸿濛。
问奇恍入娜镮地,得路疑窥碧落宫。
我亦暮年思勇退,寻源可许访仙风。

翠峰松涛

层峦叠嶂翠森森，松际涛声出茂林。
带雨萧疏寒戛玉，临风断续韵敲金。
鹤吟疑和宫商曲，鳞老犹存铁石心。
如此大材幽谷困，揖严能否遇知音。

6. 民间传说

（1）西江涤肠。

王仁裕是五代时期著名的诗人，一生写了 385 卷诗，有"诗窖子"之称。可他年轻时，家境贫寒，每天以山林为伴，砍柴度日。20 岁了还不识字。

一天，王仁裕转悠到西江祠外一块大石头上玩耍，玩着玩着，迷迷糊糊地睡着了。他飘飘忽忽来到西江岸边，看见他的身影倒映在河水中，水中的他蓬头垢面，穿着一身油渍渍的破烂衣服，难看极了，他不由得大吃一惊。突然，河心猛地跃出一个白须红脸大汉，手里握着一把明晃晃的大刀，一把将他按倒，割开了他的肚子，掏出心肝，在河里洗了又洗，一股股秽气直呛鼻孔。那个大汉洗了一阵又放入他的腹腔，王仁裕吓得舌头都缩进喉咙眼里去了。过了一会儿，他闻到一股奇香直入肺腑。睁开眼睛一看，旁边堆着几堆黄灿灿的细沙，沙子里飘着诱人的香气。他捧了几把吞下去，一转眼那几堆沙子不见了。王仁裕正觉得奇怪，河里又冒出个青面獠牙的夜叉。吓得他大叫一声，翻身跌下石头。原来是个梦。

从那天起，王仁裕变得聪颖，对书籍产生了兴趣，读书时过目不忘，下笔时文思泉涌。人们都说是西江水净化了他的肚肠。有诗为证："西江涤肠秽，吞沙成大儒。若非神力引，仍是一樵夫。"

当地人又将这个故事称为"西江感应"。

（2）诸葛亮种草。

传说诸葛亮出兵祁山，后来失败收兵。诸葛亮从失败中总结出一个重要的原因——粮草问题。祁山远离四川，山隔水阻，道路崎岖，加上敌军的袭扰，粮草供应不济，致使蜀军难以长时间屯兵，造成军事失利。

一天深夜，诸葛亮经过深思熟虑后，决定让张苞带领 20 名老练军士，去寻访当地牧马人，请教此地能否种牧草。

第二天，诸葛亮和部下正在帐中议事，忽然听到外面喧哗，他出来查看，发现山下柳林里拴着几十匹骏马，高大雄健。几个伙计和一位须发银白的老人正在跟张苞争吵。原来张苞接受任务后，清早带领士兵埋伏在通往卤城的路上，他们与老人的马群相遇，误以为是强盗，便厮打起来，一直吵吵嚷嚷，连人带马来到祁山脚下。诸葛亮向老人赔礼道歉，并说明了意图，老人介绍给诸葛亮紫花苜蓿。几天后，诸葛亮亲自来到南山下的圈马沟拜访老人。老人向诸葛亮讲述了自己的身世，老人原是马超的父亲西凉太守马腾的部下，马腾起兵讨伐曹操失败后，老人跟随马超投奔刘备，在战斗中负伤，就与孙子相依为命，在这里一面靠采集野果度日，一面种草养马。

老人把他所有的苜蓿种子全部给了诸葛亮。诸葛亮任命老人为种草督尉，拨一千军士归他指挥，专门种植苜蓿。军士们按照老人的指点，三五成群，扮作百姓的模样，分散活动，从祁山脚下到渭水两岸，只要是荒山野洼，就将苜蓿籽悄悄播种。诸葛亮在西汉水南岸军垒旁边的山坡上，亲手试种了一片，至今仍受到乡亲们特意保护，草木丛生。

魏军得知诸葛亮种草意图长久屯兵的计划后，就发动了突然袭击。祁山失守，蜀军撤退时，老人正在南山屏风峡种植苜蓿，担任掩护的张苞，一面在山顶擂鼓督战，一面催老人快走。老人却夺下鼓槌，把张苞和孙子推上战马，一声大吼，双眼圆睁，鼓声如雷。直到苜蓿种完，最后一名军士撤离，老人自己却被魏军乱箭射死。从此，人们就把这个地方叫作擂鼓坪。

（3）"雷峰夕照"的来历。

雷王庙位于礼县雷王乡，是为了纪念为百姓诊治疾病、抗旱救灾做了许多好事的雷王保。曾有几个文人学士来雷王庙玩，出了庙门，夕阳夕照，余晖彤彤，他们回头一看，只见坐落在雷王山顶的雷王大殿，香烟袅袅，紫气微微，仿佛是一片极乐净土。此景此情，使他们流连忘返，齐叹人间竟有如此美妙的景色！于是便将此景命名为"雷峰夕照"，从此"雷峰夕照"以它特有的魅力成为礼县古八景之一。

相传唐开元元年（713），唐玄宗有病，御医无法诊治，宫里大小官员急得像热锅上的蚂蚁。此时，有位原籍陇上的官员奏了一本，说是秦州城东有个雷王保，又名雷牛，已有道根，并具回天之术，请皇上恩准治病。雷王保被宣进宫后，的确身手不凡，诊脉三次，用药三回，竟药到病除。玄宗大喜，要将雷王保留在宫中。雷王保从开始学医就立志为百姓解除疾患，当然不肯留在宫中为皇上一人服务。他以家有老母妻儿为由，再三推脱，终得皇上恩准。临走时皇上封他为"盖天盖地盖国雷王"。雷王保谢恩后，生怕皇上变卦，急速踏上返乡旅途。

雷王保走后，有一个大臣向皇上进言："皇上给雷王保封得太大了，'盖天盖地盖国雷王'不是连皇上您都盖住了吗？"皇上听罢，方才醒悟，急忙命令姬、兆二位将军赶快追赶，并密言，在哪里追上，就在哪里杀掉。

雷王保行至白石镇太皇山（今雷王山）境内，掐指一算，方知有人追来，急忙撒了一把菜籽（此地现名菜籽坡），转眼长出一片绿油油的菜田，将姬、兆二位将军的马绊住，行走艰难。雷王保又走到一个大湾里，回头一看，姬、兆二位将军又追上来，雷王保又撒了一把酸刺籽（此地现名酸刺湾），酸刺呼啦啦长了起来，姬、兆二位将军的马不能前进，二人抽刀左砍右剁，好不容易砍出一条路，急忙追赶。追到一面坡上，雷王保撒了一把沙子，顿时狂风四起，飞沙走石（此地现名沙石坡），厚厚的沙石将姬、兆二位将军的马陷住，不得前进。两人好不容易打马挣扎出来，雷王保已经不见踪影。二人急忙追赶，眼看就要追上了，雷王保又朝后撒了一把黄蒿籽，眨眼间黄蒿长得一人深（此地现名庞蒿崖，庞为黄的谐音）。由于黄蒿的阻隔，雷王保才跑上了太皇山。忽见眼前横出一条大沟。他正要躲避，见姬、兆二位将军追来，雷王保急了，又撒了一把竹子籽，霎时竹子成林，将沟封严。雷王保出沟行了一段，忽听身后喊声又起，急忙把身上带的最后一把毛刺籽当空撒去（此地现名毛刺湾），转身就跑。来到一条山梁前，山梁很高，可姬、兆二位将军立马追到，雷王保急了，抽刀将山梁砍作两段（此地现名断弦子），雷王保将刀架在山梁上，刀刃朝上，姬、兆二位将军未勒住马，一个猛子冲上刀刃。雷王保喊问姬、兆二位将军："愿死还是愿活？"二人求饶，雷王将刀一翻，二人掉下深涧。脱尸后，灵魂上天为神，当地人们至今叫他们为"姬爷、兆爷"。尸体就地埋葬（此地现名坟祠）。

雷王保不再打算回家，他知道朝廷还会加害于他，于是便在太皇山住下来，炼丹修道（此地现名洞崖下，炼丹的洞至今还在），采集白药为当地百姓诊治疾病。雷王保晒药的地方至今还在，人们叫它"晒药场"。

太皇山从此就叫雷王山。

7. 新闻报道

西汉水悠唱千古英雄　秦文化续写崭新篇章
—— 秦始皇老家的惊人发现

庞世栋

礼县，是一处古老而神奇的地方，是一片创造辉煌和缔造伟业的热土。这里的史前文化、先秦文化和三国文化遗址星罗棋布，灿若群星。地处县城东部、依山傍水的大堡子山就是镶嵌在这块热土上的一颗璀璨明珠。随着国家考古工作的逐步进行，新发掘的城址、祭祀坑、青铜编钟和其他考古成果，让这颗"明珠"更加耀眼夺目，让世人注目，让海内外震惊。

据考证，秦国共有四大陵园区，1987年前第二、三、四陵园区的位置陆续确定，即陕西省的雍城陵区（西陵）、芷阳陵区（东陵）和秦始皇陵园。但第一陵园在何处却一直是困扰史学界和考古学界的千古之谜。1993年在礼县城东13公里的永兴乡大堡子山一带，发现了秦贵族和秦公两大墓葬区，经国内考古界、史学界专家研究考证，被确认为秦四大陵园中的第一大陵园，即"秦西垂陵园"，墓群范围为东西6千米、南北3千米，总面积18平方千米。当时清理墓葬14座，车马坑2座，出土文物300多件，包括鼎、簋、壶等大型青铜礼器及金器等。发掘了两座南北并列的"中"字形和"目"字形墓葬，规模宏大，总长度分别为88米和115米，其中有"秦公作铸用鼎"和"秦公铸用簋"铭文字样的青铜器。经专家考证，初步确定为秦襄公夫妇或其子秦文公夫妇的陵墓。因此，这里被史学界确定为秦公陵园而轰动国内外，从而揭开了几千年来中国和世界历史学界和考古学界的一大奇谜。十年来，国内考古专家、学者和日本等国的史学家先后来到礼县进行早期秦文化的调查、考古、发掘和研究。经过考古、发掘和研究论证，礼县太堡子山发现的古墓群被专家一致认定为秦始皇祖先的第一大陵园——西垂陵园，礼县是秦"西犬丘（西垂）"所在地。有关专家认为，"秦西垂园陵的发掘，是二十世纪继敦煌藏经洞和兵马俑之后的又一大发现"，对研究先秦时期的政治、经济、军事、文化、冶金、铸造、礼制、陵寝制度等方面有着不可估量的历史价值和学术价值，填补了先秦文化研究的空白。北京大学考古系主任高崇文教授指出："这是对早期秦文化考古具有突破性的重大发现，更为重要的是这一发现在礼县，必将揭开早期秦都城遗址之谜。"

近十年来，礼县县委、县政府在省、市领导和国家、省文物局的大力支持下，紧紧围绕秦公陵园遗址的保护、利用，做了不懈努力，先后召开了"全国秦人西垂文化座谈会"，还在北京大学赛克勒考古与艺术博物馆举办了"甘肃省礼县秦西垂陵区青铜器特展"，使秦公陵园遗址誉满华夏、驰名海外。1997年，甘肃省人民政府将礼县大堡子山秦公墓地列为全省重点文物保护单位，并公布了大堡子山秦公墓地保护范围。2001年7月，该墓地又被国务院正式列为全国第五批文物保护单位。为了更好地对该遗址进行保护和开发利用，2002年礼县又委托陕西省古建筑设计研究院完成了秦公陵园遗址保护的综合规划，并同时邀请陕西、甘肃两省考古界、建筑界专家，经实地考察后，召开了"大堡子山遗址及墓群保护规划论证会"，通过这次省级论证后报请国家文物局批准实施。这标志着不久的将来，秦早期都城、居址、建筑、铸造、礼制、陵寝等早期秦文化将会栩栩如生地展现在世人面前，重放异彩。

早期秦文化研究是一项系统工程，工作量大，牵涉面广，在国家文物局、省文物局的大力支持下，于2004年3月由省文物考古研究所、陕西省考古研究所、中国国家博物馆、北京大学考古文博学院、西北大学考古系5家单位组成了联合考古队，并成立早期秦文化研究课题组，计划在五年时间内对秦人早期活动地域的西汉水流域、渭河上游及其支流进行较大规模的考古调查、发掘以及综合性的研究。

据文献记载，西汉水流域是秦人早期活动的中心区域，秦公大墓的发现证实了这一点。联合考古队首先把工作重点放在了西汉水流域。考古队员们对东起天水市的天水乡、西至礼县的江口乡，长约40千米的西汉水干流两岸地区以及红河、水坪河、燕子河等支流地域进行了系统的踏勘，10位专业人员分为2组，走遍了西汉水两岸的每座山头、每块台地，调查了各时期的古代遗址。三年来，经过考古工作者艰辛的调查、考古、钻探和发掘，目前，早期秦文化考古工作取得了阶段性重大成果，又一次震惊了海内外。

联合考古队的甘肃省文物考古研究所副所长王辉说，通过对礼县西汉水及其支流的考察，考古队发现了大量的周秦时期秦人相关遗存。共发现各类遗址98处，新发现70余处遗址。在调查的47处周代遗址中，以秦文化为主的遗址38处，其中"六八图—费家庄""大堡子山—赵坪""雷神庙（西山）—石沟坪"三个相对独立又互有联系的大遗址群，可以说是早期秦人活动的三个中心区。西汉水流域的文物考古调查，为探索一些历史上悬而未决的问题，比如秦早期都邑"西犬丘"、秦文化的形成，以及秦、戎关系等，提供了重要的线索。同时，考古队还在县城西山、大堡子山和山坪发现了三处西周到春秋时期的城址。西山城址依山而建，目前已发现的各段城墙总长约1 200米，废弃年代不晚于春秋早期。同时，考古队发现墓葬800座，还有房屋基址、灰坑、古道路、窑址等遗迹，基本了解了西山遗址和城址的范围、结构和布局。

　　位于县城城西的鸾亭山汉代祭祀遗址的发现是早期秦文化考古工作中的又一个重要成果。遗址由海拔1 700米的鸾亭山山顶的祭祀台和山腰的东西夯土台组成。附近发现有周代祭祀坑、战国汉代墓葬80多座。发掘出土了祭祀用玉、长乐未央瓦当和兽骨等，该遗址在周代就有人类居住、活动。在一条东西长约20米的汉代半月形浅沟内清理出11套组合完整的玉器，共51件，器类有圭、璧、玉人三种。组合方式有圭压璧的，有璧压圭的，也有多件玉璧上下叠压的。玉圭最大的直径长约15厘米，宽约10厘米；玉璧最大的直径约22厘米。圭多青玉，璧多白玉。玉人两件，一男一女，与圭、璧共出。《觐礼》曰："四圭尺寸有二，以祀天。"又曰"以苍璧礼天，以黄琮礼地。"该遗址应是汉代一个专门的祭天祭祀场所，为研究汉代郊祀用玉及相关礼制提供了重要的考古学资料。

　　今年来，通过调查发现，在10平方千米的范围内分布有大堡子山城址、山坪城址以及圆顶山、盐土崖两处贵族墓地。大堡子遗址总面积约50万平方米，除少量的齐家文化遗存外，主体为周代城址、城外墓葬和居址、东城外中小型墓地、中心区的秦公大墓及祭祀坑等几部分。城址建在山坡上，平面大致呈长方形，有夯土城墙，夯土城墙东、西两道长1 000米，北城墙长约250米，南墙尚未发现。城墙夯筑，北墙保存情况最好，方向45度。城址内面积约25万平方米，秦公大墓、火型建筑基址、祭祀坑均包括在内。城内外遗址目前已钻探面积129万平方米。目前为止，共发现各类遗迹699处，有夯土城墙、建筑基址、灰坑、陶窑、墓葬、水井、车马坑等。2006年在大堡子山遗址上已发掘探明规模最大的一座建筑基址，南北长102米，东西宽17米，建筑基址四周为夯土围墙，中间有17个大型柱础石，西墙地面以上残高20至60厘米，墙宽1.5米左右，地下基础宽约3米，东墙、北墙以及南墙东半部只剩地基部分，宽2至3米左右。该建筑规模宏大，当为大型宫殿类建筑。从地层堆积和夯土内的包含物看，这座建筑基址大约始建于西周晚期、春秋初期，战国时期被废弃，汉代遭到严重破坏。现代因修整梯地，东墙地上部分完全被毁。已发掘墓葬6座，车马坑1座，人祭坑4座，器物坑1座，清理出土了青铜钟、石磬。刚刚发掘出的祭祀坑，专家推测可能是用于祭祀地神，此次发掘中出土的文物中最引人瞩目的是一套秦早期的青铜编钟，由3个大钟和8个小钮钟组成，外观完整，整体呈现深绿色，11个钟一字排开，整齐地摆放在坑道里。考古学家说，这套编钟保存得非常完好，完全出土后，仍然可以再一次演奏出美妙的音乐来。

通过这次调查、钻探和发掘，考古队基本了解了大堡子山遗址的布局和结构。大堡子山遗址发掘发现的有夯土墙和柱础的大型宫殿式建筑以及出土青铜编钟的祭祀坑，对认识大堡子城址的性质、确认秦公大墓的墓主和研究当时的祭祀及礼乐制度、铜器铸造工艺等提供了极为珍贵的资料。同时，也为大堡子山遗址的保护和利用提供了科学依据。

大堡子山遗址新发掘出土的周代城址和居址、城外墓地、青铜编钟、祭祀坑等一批国宝级珍贵文物源于西周时期到春秋时期。其规模之大，规格之高，实属罕见。据司马迁的《史记·秦本纪》记载，秦人在西周时期主要活动于今甘肃东南部，而其都邑"西犬丘"（西垂）及先公陵墓则在今礼县的西汉水上游一带，由此证实司马迁的记载是可信的。同时，本次发掘，第一次揭露出大规模的早期秦人聚落遗存，为了解秦人当时的居住形态等取得了新资料。通过这些大量的周秦时期和秦人相关的遗存，进一步证明了礼县是早期秦人活动的中心地区，是秦汉时期的西县所在地，是秦先祖、秦文化的真正发祥地，是千古一帝秦始皇的"老家"。

早期秦文化考古项目，是我国新世纪的一项重大文化工程。礼县是中华民族的发祥地之一，历史悠久，古迹众多，地域文化遗产丰富独特。我们有理由相信，联合考古队在未来的考古发掘工作中，可能还会有更大的收获，让"历史的记忆"震惊世人。

（选自《陇南报》2006年11月25日 周末特刊）

Chapter One   Introduction of Lixian

1. A Brief Survey of Lixian

Lixian, Which was called Xichui, Xiquanqiu or Lancang in the ancient time, lies in the northern part of Longnan city, in the southeast of Gansu province. It has a long history with a splendid culture. The mountains and rivers in Lixian are elegant with plentiful natural resources. It has long been called "An important birth place of Qin people, and the battlefield of the Three kingdoms Period".

Coming over to Lixian, you will find it is an old mysterious place. It has been shown by un-earthed artifacts, that as early as the late Neolithic Age, over 6,000 years ago, our forefathers were living here. They created a splendid historic civilization. The Ba-Shu culture along Changjiang River and the Yangshao culture along the Yellow River were mixed here because of its special geographic position. The long-standing civilization here was pregnant with Lixian's unique form of culture, such as, The Yangshao culture, the former Qin Dynasty's culture, and the Three Kingdoms Period's culture. Many famous historical figures were living here, among them, Zhao Yi, a famous poet and composer in the Eastern Han Dynasty; Wang Renyu, a well-known poet at the Five Dynasties Period; Zhao Shiyan, a Prime Minister in the Yuan Dynasty; and Men Kexin, an eminent minister of Rituals in the Ming Dynasty. What's more, many places of historic interest and scenic sites are kept very well. Among them the most famous are, Dabuzi Mountain's Qingongs' Tombs, the Xichui Funerary Tombs, Qi Mountain Zhuge Liang Temple, one of the five greatest Zhuge Liang temples in all, the Ancestral Temple over the Salt Well, where a famous poet of the

Tang Dynasty once composed a poem, Tielong Mountain, where Jiangwei, an eminent general of the Three Kingdoms Period fought against Sima Zhao, a general of the Wei kingdom of the same dynasty.

Lixian has an area of about 4,300 square kilometers and a population of 520,000. It has not only a splendid culture, but also plentiful natural resources. The Chinese herb, rhubarb, which is grown at Quanshui in Lixian has a good reputation all over the world. It has long been known that "Chinese rhubarb is a good one in the world, and Quanshui rhubarb is the best." The volume of export was 56 percent of the nation's export in the 1980s.

Lixian is one of the China's 32 good quality apple-growing regions, and also the Bapan pear, one of the famous pears, is produced. The total area of growing apples trees is over 300,000 mu[①]. And the annual output of fresh apples is more than 20,000 tons. Aslo, there are other famous agriculture products such as wild pepper and wild vegetables. Among mineral resources gold and silver are the most famous .

The seasons in Lixian are different from each other. Its annual average temperature is 9 degrees centigrade. Many plants usually found in most regions grow well in this area. Wheat, corn, and potatoes are the major crops. Tobacco grown here also enjoys a good reputation throughout the nation. Lixian is rich in natural mineral resources. With its mild climate and plentiful rainwater, its forests cover 1,250,000 mu. Forest cover is 21 percent, leaving 1,700,000 mu land for growing crops or planting grass. Animal husbandry is also developed. Thousands of farm animals are bought and sold at the famous livestock marketplace in Yanguan town, the largest in Northwest China.

Since the Policy of Reform and Opening has been carried on, the hardworking and honest people in Lixian generate wealth through their own efforts and smooth away difficulties so that the economy and every social enterprise are developing rapidly. Basic infrastructure sections, like

---

① 1mu≈666.7 m^2

communications and transport, education and health, are developing well day by day. The people here are not only good and honest, but also modest and eager to learn. Since the people and government attach great importance to education, those of talent are encouraged and developed. The level of urbanization is improving continuously. Comprehensive economic strength of Lixian is increasing constantly. As the feature production of agriculture is believed firmly as a base, gold mining, other local industries trade and tourism have become the main body of the local economy. Thus the pattern of the balanced development of agriculture, industry and tertiary industries has been formed, too. Looking forward to the future, Lixian, which has a long history and in consequence quite a few sites of ancient culture, will own a wonderful and splendid prosperity. It is believed that with the on-going strategy of developing Western China, by the people's hard work and with the cooperation of men of insight all over the world, the future is looking bright!

2. Position, Population and Nationalities

Lixian county is in the southern part of Longnan city, which is located in the southeast of Gansu province. It is 345 kilometers from Lanzhou. It borders on the locations of Gangu and Wushan in the north, Tianshui and Xihe in the east, Wudu in the south, Tanchang and Mingxian in the west. The climate and soil of Lixian are suitable for animal husbandry and agriculture. The whole county covers an area of 4,299.92 square kilometers.

Lixian now manages 34 villages and 2 towns. It has a total population of more than 500,000 with six nationalities including Han, Hui, Manchu, Tibetan, Mongolian, Tujia. 98% of population are Han, and 1.5% are Hui. Others include Tibetan, Man, Mongolian, Tujia.

3. Historical Evolution

Because this region has a mild climate and fertile land, there are rivers, forests, and mountains. It meets the conditions for ancient human habitation. According to records, the area has been populated for several thousand years, and there are many remains of primitive societies, including the Former Qin and Yangshao cultures of the Neolithic Age. So Lixian has a long history, and can be named "the birth place of the Qin people". As early as the Neolithic Age, 6,000 years ago, human beings had settled the reaches of the Xihan River.

In the Xia and Shang Dynasties (2100—1100 BC), The Di and Qiang people hunted and lived here.

During the Qin Dynasty (221—206 BC), It was subordinate to Xi county, Longxi prefecture.

During the Three Kingdoms Period (220—280 AD), the northeast part of it was subordinate to Xi county, Tianshui prefecture of the Wei kingdom, and the southwest part to Wudu county, Wudu prefecture of the Shu kingdom.

During the Northern Wei Dynasty (386—534 AD), it was named Lancang, Hanyang Prefecture, Southern Qin state.

During the Northern Song Dynasty (960—1127 AD), it was divided into two parts, one was Changdao county; the other was Datan county. Both were in the Ming prefecture.

In the ninth year of Chenghua, Ming Dynasty (1473 AD), it began to be called Lixian, subordinated to Gongchang Official Government, the Qin prefecture.

On August 11, 1949, it was liberated by the PLA; Wudu prefecture had jurisdiction over it. In 1955, Tianshui prefecture administered it. In 1958, Lixian and Xihe made a new county named Xili county. In January 1962, the former organizational system was restored. In June 1986, it was also designated to Longnan city.

4. Society, Economy and Resources

Lixian has abounding natural resources. There are six major resources. The first one is the mineral, of which gold is the main one, the second one is the Chinese medicinal herbs, such as, rhubarb, licorice root, milk vetch (both red and yellow) and so on. Because of the mild climate and good soil, it is neither too cold in winter nor too hot in summer. Most of the land is suitable for animal husbandry. In fact, besides poultry and livestock, there are also wild animals. They form the third major resource. The fourth is trees, including apple-trees, Chinese prickly ash trees, walnut trees and so on. The fifth is hydropower resources. The sixth is, the tourism resources, which are based on the sites of the ancient Yangshao, the Former Qin Dynasty and the Three Kingdoms Period cultures.

Lixian is an agricultural county with local medium and small sized industries and some tertiary industries as supplementary. So, in addition to agriculture, Lixian also stresses forestry, animal husbandry, industry and tourism. With the policy of Reform and Opening and the strategy of Developing Western China being carried out, the economy and all enterprises are making great progress. The process of modernization is speeding up. Science and technology, education, culture and health all have realized marked development. The basic infrastructures are being perfected, such as, transportation and communication and electric power, etc. The people's material and cultural levels are being raised step by step. The standard of urbanization is constantly improving. The structure of production is rationalized as well. As a result, Lixian has changed from a large resource and population county to a tourism and economy one.

Chapter Two Scenic Spots

1. Dabuzi Mountain's Qingongs' Funerary Park

Lixian county, was called Xichui or Xiquanqiu, Which is the ancient birth place of the Qin people, the earliest capital of the Qin Dynasty (221-206BC). Historically the former ancestors of the Qin people resided in Xiquanqiu. Qinzhong, Zhuanggong and Xianggong were buried here. It was once a cradle in which they set up their own power. The reason that the forefathers of the Qin people originated here and built the capital here as well is simple and clear.

It is said that the Qin people came from Shandong at the end of the Shang Dynasty, the chief led the troops to the middle reaches of the Wei River and guarded the border area of the Shang Dynasty. When the Zhou people had destroyed the Shang's Power, the Zhou people occupied the district. Daluo, one of Qin's chiefs, led them to search for a place along the Wei River where they could live. At last they got to the upper reaches of the Xihan River (Xihan shui), far away from the center of Zhou Power. As a result, they preserved a relatively Independent society that laid a foundation for their developing and strengthening. Later on, just in this place they defeated the Di people who were weaker than their own and built cities. After the Zhou Dynasty was founded, they put themselves in the King of Zhou's charge. The King approved that they could capture Xiquanqiu and affirmed their social position. One of the Qin people's forefathers, Feizi, was good at raising horses, which was recognized the worth of dependency. So his son was an honored official, after Qinzhong died in a war fighting the Rong people, his son Zhuanggong continued fighting them and recovered the lost territories. He made himself a local official in Xichui. The younger sons,

Zhuanggong and Xianggong once escorted the King of Zhou to move the capital to Luoyi. He was also an honored high official, because of his meritorious service, and a Prefecture was founded. Wengong inherited the throne and went on fighting the Rong people, and captured Qi Mountain (Qishan) in Shaanxi province. From then on they began to lead a life of going in for agriculture when finishing their nomadic life, with the Primitive society turning into the Serf System. The Qin came to a real state and strengthened and developed in Xichui.

At the beginning of the 1990s, it is at Dabuzi Mountain that people have unearthed Four Large scale Cemeteries during the Qin Dynasty, and excavated unmatched, extremely rare relics, therefore it is well known at home and abroad. There are 300 cultural relics that ranked at first level in the state. After analysis and research of the unearthed artifacts, experts preliminarily maintained that it was the tomb of Qinzhong, Zhuanggong or Xianggong, and established this cemetery to be the first funerary park in the Qin Dynasty (221—206 BC). It caused a great sensation in historical-philosophical and archaeological circles. Li Xueqing, who is a member of experts group of the project to divide Xia, Shang, Zhou Dynasties by period, points out, Lixian is the birth place of the Qin people, it plays an important part in the ancient historical civilization of China, It is helpful to the courses of the archaeological circle and also historical research. The vice director of the cultural relics archaeological institute, Cao Wei, said, two great archeological discoveries of cultural relics in Gansu this century, one is the Cave of Dunhuang, the other is the Qingong Tomb at Dabuzi Mountain in Lixian.

The protection and exploitation of the Qingong funerary park has aroused great concern in various circles of society. The exploitation plan has been finished by ancient architectural research institute of Shaanxi Province, and passed the appraisal of experts. In the near future, the primitive style of Xichui funerary park of the Qin Dynasty will reappear for scholars and tourists at home or abroad to visit, for the archaeology as well.

2. Xichui Museum of the Qin Dynasty in Lixian

The museum was set up on the western street, which is the pubic center of culture and entertainment. It attracted many more visitors for the rare relics. The total amount of unearthed relics is about 15 kinds with 3,000 pieces. Such as, fossils, stone artifacts, bone artifacts, pottery, china ware, bronze articles, iron ware, jade articles, gold objects or silver ware, ancient coins, brick carving, wood carving, calligraphy and painting, historical data and so on. Among them, over 100 are class A cultural property under national protection, while the others are under provincial and county's protection. It is believed that it's a relics treasure house for people to study the Yangshao, Former Qin and Three Kingdoms cultures. Some of them were once displayed at Beijing University in the year of 2000. Thousands of historians and archaeologists were attracted. At the present, with as much as 14 yuan million being invested, a new construction with carved beams and painted rafters will appear in the world, it will also receive more and more domestic and foreign visitors.

3. Zhuge Liang Temple at Qi Mountain

Qi Mountain village (Qi shan) is between Yanguan on the east and Dabuzi Mountain on the west. But Qi Mountain is located at the northern bank of the Xihan River, about 25 kilometers east of Lixian county town. Once it was the key passage to Sichuan from Gansu, which was easy to defend and difficult to attack. It seemed to be a natural barrier in the ancient wars, so for it was fought as a strategic point by both the Wei Kingdom and the Shu Kingdom. Zhuge Liang, the Prime Minister of the Shu Kingdom sent troops to Qi Mountain six times. With the TV play, the Romance of "Three Kingdoms", having been on, Qi Mountain is also known to all, the temple has been a famous scenic spot as well.

In March of the fifth year of Jianxing(227 AD), Zhuge Liang presented credentials to the King, Liu Shan, then he dispatched troops to Hanzhong and founded a provisional ministry. In April of the next year (228 AD), he led his troops to Qi Mountain for the first time, but they were defeated. In tears Zhuge Liang executed general Ma Su. In the winter of the same year, he came to Qi Mountain for a second time. Although his soldiers encircled Chencang, they still had to be dismissed because of the shortage of supplies. For a third time in the seventh year of the reign of Jianxing (229 AD), the general of the Shu Kingdom, Chengshi, occupied Wudu and Yinping, Zhuge Liang himself got to Jianwei town (in Xihe county). In the following year (230 AD), another famous general of the Shu Kingdom, Wei Yan, entered Tianshui in the west and defeated Guo Huai, a general of the Wei Kingdom. That was the fourth time. In the ninth year (231 AD), he, together with his troops, reached Qi Mountain yet again. Zhuge Liang withdrew the troops as Li Yan lied about the situation of the troops. The fifth time was not any success. The last time for him to dispatch troops to Qi Mountain was in the twelfth year of Jianxing (234 AD). More than ten thousand soldiers went into the battle, Zhuge Liang stationed troops in Wuzhangyuan. It was in August of this year that Zhuge Liang passed away. In fact, for these six times Zhuge Liang dispatched troops to Qi Mountain, only twice did he himself arrive there; twice he was near to it, and the other times he did not reach it at all. His arriving at Qi Mountain for six times was just a part of his northern punitive expedition. That was also a symbol of his spirit. "Bending himself a task and exerting himself to the utmost, and go on up to the death".

  The Qi Mountain Fortress is located in the middle part of the Village, on the right bank of Xihan River. It is a solitary hill of which the framework is stones and earth; the shape looks just like a tortoise or a ship. The Zhuge Liang Temple stands on the top of it. According to legend, it was there since the Jin Dynasty, one of the Five Great Zhuge Liang Temples throughout China, which was protected well for a long time. Local people hold a memorial ceremony for him at times. So it is made to be wonderful and worth visiting.

  If you come over to the fortress, there will stand a mountain in front you before you see it. With steep hillside and unique shape, you must mistake it for a ship on the sea. Going up the steps, you will find some displays, such as some famous paintings and handwritings, the words, Wu Hou Ancestral Temple comes into your eyes, which was written by a well-known calligrapher, Gu Zihui. On both sides of the gate is the famous article, "Manuscript of Dispatching Troops to Fight (Chushibiao)" carved on stones, you can't help thinking of the spirit of Zhuge Liang. Entering the gate, you will see Kongming Palace, Guanyu (a famous general in Shu Kingdom) and Ti Buddha Halls, which were first constructed in the Western or Eastern Jin Dynasties, and rebuilt in the Ming and the Qing Dynasties. The figure of Zhuge Liang was molded in the year of Daoguang of Qing Dynasty. That the sculpture was made of wood and clay is gilded and painted and is exquisite, well proportioned and natural looking. Zhuge Liang was sitting in a special chair with a feather fan in his hand, which looks like a real. Here the status gallery of generals and officials in the war are on show in the temples. These detailed and vivid pictures are of great historic and artistic value.

In the temple there are many steles with various inscriptions, including 30 plaques and silk banners embroidered with words of praise, 5 pairs of couplets, 20 inscribed stone tablets. Among them, both "Climbing Qi Mountain to Visit Wuhou Temple" composed by Zheng Guoshi, a governor of Zhejiang in the Ming Dynasty, and the inscription on a tablet, "Looking Far into the Distance at Qi Mountain" written by Wang Hua'nan in the Chinese cursive hand, are the admiration of every visitor. So it is also valuable from the aspect of literature and calligraphy.

If you stand on the top of the fortress, all the ancient battlegrounds lie before your eyes. On the northeast there is Tianshui Pass, the Ancestral Temple over Salt Wells, the Lane of Wood Gate, A Long-snake Battle Formation of Jiugudui; on the south there is the Enclosing Horses Gully and Hiding Soldiers Bend. According to legend, there was a huge natural cave leading to the Xihan River. It was an ancient passage used for drawing water by the soldiers of Shu Kingdom. It is said that it was just the cave that Zhuge

Liang himself came in and went out through when he made his rounds in the campsite. There is a large stone in the middle of the river, which was used to mount a horse by Zhuge Liang. While you are looking at the martyrs' temple and recalling the history, you might feel that you are in the ancient battlefront, thrilling and marvelous, boundless and distant.

4. Ancestral Temple over the Salt Well

Yanguan, was called " the City of Salt" in ancient times and has a long history. It is the eastern gate of Lixian, and a very important town as well. The salt well lies outside the southern gate of the town seat, near the Livestock Marketplace, which was first started by the Qin people in the Zhou Dynasty. Later on, the government was set up to manage the salt production. As salt was produced for many years, the name of the government became the name of place. Salt production has been an important handicraft since it was opened on. As a result, it was also a main source of the local people's income. Local people who produced salt from wells were as many as 300 households in the 1950s. The annual output of salt was as much as 400,000 kilograms. When the salted soil was cooked on the fire, the valley was full of the smoke.

According to *The Historical Records*, Feizi lived in Quanqiu (in the eastern part of Lixian). He was fond of horses and good at raising them. This was told to King of Zhou so that the King made him live between the Jing River and the Wei River in order to breed horses. The Qin people living here did well in raising horses and were appreciated by the king of Zhou. Hence they got the surname "Ying" from the King. Horses were bred very well, thus showing that the water with salt played an important part, as also their good methods and abundant waterweeds. Because horses drink it, they would grow fast and strong. Therefore horses raised in Yanguan are well known all over the country. Nowadays the Livestock Marketplace has become the largest in Northwest China.

The salt here has a medicinal function. It can be used for curing arthritis or other diseases with great effect. The Ancestral Temple over a Salt Well, which was established in the Zhou Dynasty is protected perfectly. The depth of the well is about 17 meters. The mouth is a square shape with each side being 127 centimeters. Till now the water, full of salt, is still overflowing. The tools, which were used to cook salt, are fully equipped. Dedications and poems written by scholars and poets of the Tang and later Dynasties are carved on stone tablets or walls increasing the value of the ancestral temple for literary and historical study. Being worth mentioning is "The Poem about the Salt Wells" composed by Du Fu, a famous poet, on his way to Sichuan during the Tang Dynasty.

The God Temple was made up of three rooms. The God was an old woman (salt grand mother). According to legend, the old man (salt grandfather) is worshipped in another temple at Yanchuan village in Zhangxian county. Because there was no salt water in the wells in every other year, the people in the ancient times always said they had been making an appointment and the God was not here. Tofu, made with this kind of salt, tastes rare and crisp, and looks bright and full of luster. If you come here, you should have it. It will make you aftertaste forever.

The Yanguan salt wells were closely related with the civilization of Qin Dynasty's production and development, the Qin people exploited the salt wells, which laid a foundation for the economical development. So it is believed that before long the salt culture should merge in the world as an important part of the Qin culture

5. An Ecological Scenic Spot of the Great Fragrant Mountain (Xiangshan)

Xiangshan is located 50 kilometers south of Lixian. With an elevation of 2,532 meters, it is just on the border area of Lixian and Xihe counties. According to Xiangshan biography, it was the place where Miaoshan practiced Buddhism, who was King Miaozhuang's third daughter of the Xinglin Kingdom. It has been famous for its well-known and grand temples since ancient times, and was the Holy land of Taoism from the beginning of the Han Dynasty and was supplemented by the latecomers.

Xiangshan used to be covered with towering cypresses, pines and other trees. But in 1958, it was destroyed. At the end of 1982, a great plan of flying planting trees was carried out. And then dibble seeding and scatter seeding with the areas by 260,000 mu. The destroyed-temples were also rebuilt in 1983. Today, there are many scenic spots, such as, Tiger Hole, Silent Spring, Nodding Tree, Ice Cave, Sister Stones and Sacrificing Cliff, all attracting sightseers from different places usually on the eighth of April till the fifth of May in the Chinese lunar calendar. At that time, the Buddhist temples and Taoist mansions really give the impression of an enchanted land.

The best time to visit the Xiangshan is on April eighth of the Chinese lunar calendar, because it is the day of the Great Mountain Temple Fair. At that time the mountain has just begun to put on its spring finery, very often it is warm and sunny and colorful butterflies flit about. The people from all directions come to enjoy sweet flowers and singing birds. Buddhists gather to attend special service in the temple. Inside the temple joss sticks burn, outside vendors hawk their small commodities. This usually tranquil Buddhist and Taoist retreat becomes an exciting place full of life.

6. Ancient Battleground–Tielong Mountain

This is located on the Northern bank of Xihan River, 15 kilometers southwest from Lixian county town. Walking along the Shi-Cao Road to the south (from Shiqiao to Caoping) you will see a mountain standing before you, with precipitous hillsides and some rapids. It looks like a bottle upside-down. The torrent rushes through the valley, which sounds like thunder. It was called Tielong Mountain because it was like a big birdcage. Here once was an ancient battlefield, when the General of Shu Kingdom, Jiangwei and his troops were stationed here and fought against Sima Zhao (the minister of Wei Kingdom). It is said that Sima Zhao's troops were besieged and they were hungry and thirsty, suddenly a fountain issued form and saved his troops. Till today the spring still flows from the mountain. In the mountain, Sima's seal, head of arrow, dagger-axes and large spears were unearthed.

7. Forest Region of Taoping

This is located 75 kilometers southeast of Lixian county town, in Shangping village. There is a virgin forest with varies of wild plants and many kinds of wild animals. More than 300 species of woody plant together with 50 kinds of animals are found in this region. Among them are the rare animals, such as, musk, horse-like musk, black goats, golden pheasants with red feathers, leopards, antelope, deer, bear, it is also rich in wild medicinal herbs, the most famous are rhubarb, milk vetch, codonopsis pilosula, angelic root and so on. The mountains have different shapes: some look like the wheat straw piles, some like the steamed-bread, others just like stony-board, steep and dangerous. The limpid and clear brooks flow through brush and over stones. There are many waterfalls. A pleasant, still place is for the ordinary visitors. There is a valley with steep cliffs and fantastically shaped peaks on both sides. Visitors can see dense forests with countless grotesque rocks, exotic flowers and rare trees. Striking vistas constantly emerge. There are too many beautiful things for the eye to take in. So most of the scenic spots are worth visiting, especially, Big Treasure Mountain (Dabao Mountain), Mouth of the Vase (Baopingkou), and Double Towers Cliff (Shuangtaya).

8. Grasslands of Dahebian

The grasslands are also in Shangping village, with an area of as much as 200 thousand mu. There the rainwater is plentiful, and the grass is luxuriant. Herds of cattle and flocks of sheep can be seen here and there. Thousands of herdsmen coming from Gannan and Longnan have been living on the grasslands. If you get there, some well-trained horses are ready for you. They will warmly welcome you and will provide you with what you need. If you ride a horse, you can indulge your thoughts and feelings, and enjoy the grasslands' fine scenery. You can also experience personally the hard life led by the local herdsmen. You will experience the wildlife and feel close to the Land.

9. Honghe Reservoir

The Reservoir is located at Shuangshi ditch in Honghe village, 40 kilometers northeast from Lixian county town. It is a middle-sized reservoir. It can be used to irrigate, to breed fish and to control floods, to visit and go sightseeing. It was started in December 1957, and finished in January 1959. Since it was set up, the reservoir, in addition to developing its function that it should have, the scenery has attracted a large number of travelers. On the weekends or holidays, visitors come here to boat or fish or have a swim and make the still reservoir much noisy and uncommon prosperous.

10. An Ecological Scenic Spot of the Emerald Mount Temple

As one of the eight ancient scenic spots, Cuifeng Temple lies 7.5 kilometers southeast of Lixian county town. On the mountain are dense pines and skyscraping, sturdy cypresses, fresh flowers and green lawns, soaring peaks and sharp cliffs, all of which make the place secluded and full of quiet mystery. It is not known today when the temple was built. Most of it seems to be built in the sky. The Sound of Pines on Cuifeng is one of the eight scenic spots. The gentle breeze soughs through the pines and causes the trees to sway like the waves of a green lake. There is an ancient stele, but we cannot really read it because of its having been seriously damaged at some time in the past. If we pour some water on it, we can see some dim handwriting. According to this, we know that the temple was constructed in six years by Zhanli from Zhejiang, on the 20th of leap February in the Chinese lunar calendar of the first year of Tianqi, Southern Dynasty.

In 1958, many ancient towering trees were cut down and the forests were destroyed for steel-made. As a result, the images of Buddha and the temple were damaged. Recently, people rebuilt the temple and went on planting trees on the mountain, there appears a match beauty far over what it used to be, some temples are perched on the cliffs, touching the sky, over-looking ditches, and surrounded by a paradise of trees and flowers. So now it is a good place for tourists to go to.

11. Golden Temple

This temple lies at Youhao village in Yongxing, Lixian county. The Buddhist Association of Lixian was founded in it. There is no record when it was constructed. According to legend, there once were many Buddhist monks and nuns, as well as a large number of Buddhist Nunneries and Temples, these were destroyed during the Ming Dynasty. But local people used to plough the fields there and found not only small pieces of brick and rubble debris but also the pillars of the temples in the 1990s. Some hermits who believed in Buddha raised money and rebuilt it in 1989. At the same time, the Buddhist Association of Lixian moved into this temple. Now it occupies an area of 3,000 square meters, including two halls, a Hufa hall, the great gate and 24 monks rooms.16 Buddhists and over 40 Hermits are making a life here. With the Organization being founded, both the monks and nuns go in for growing crops and publicizing the Party's religious policies. As a matter of fact, they have made a great contribution to the common religious activities and to the unity of nationalities and the stability of society.

12. Taiping Mountain Park

Located 1 kilometer north of Yanguan town, Taiping Mountain Park is a wonderful place for Taoists and visitors. It has a rational composition with the varied shapes of trees. Among the many big old-aged trees, "the cypress embraced by a pagoda" is a unique scenic spot. People from Lixian county town, Xihe county and Tianshui city pay religious homage to it on the first and the fifteenth days of every month in the Chinese lunar calendar. As a result, there is a thriving and prosperous sight.

13. Miaohe Reservoir

Located 30 kilometers north of Lixian county town, Miaohe reservoir is the most popular place of entertainment for the local people. The area always get much attention, and so it must be exciting, entertaining and must provide some pleasure as well, for there the air is fresh and clean, and there is plenty of peace and quiet. Although it is a lesser scale reservoir, the construction was started in April 1974 and finished in September 1976. It is put a good use for irrigating, controlling floods, breeding fish and generating electric power. The total surface of water is 500 mu with a volume of 8 million cubic meters. The installed capacity of the power station is 500 kW, the annual output of fish is over 2 thousand kilograms. The buildings of the whole construction are scattered here and there according to the natural relief. The river has formed 9 river bends. There boating on the man-made lake, you may mistake it for the Three Gorges of the Changjiang River. On both sides of it are soaring peaks and sharp cliffs. They are covered with green pines and cypresses in various shapes as well as other species of commercial timber. Because of its matchless beauty, millions of visitors are attracted here for various reasons.

14. Ancestral Temple Stele of Zhao Shiyan

The stele is situated only half a kilometer south of Lixian county town, in the ruins of the ancestral temple of Zhao Shiyan. It is a stele of 3.5 meters high, 1.3 meters wide and 0.24 meters thick, consisting of a Dragon Head, Stele Body and Tortoise Pedestal. It was erected in the third year of Yanyou in the Yuan Dynasty (1316 AD).

The inscription on the stone tablet was composed by Cheng Jufu, and written and cut by the famous calligrapher, Zhao Mengfu as an imperial order. There are 1,230 characters all together, incised script around the front and regular script in the middle, which consist of 33 lines of vertical strokes with 64 characters each. They are the records of the six heroes' contribution of Zhao Shiyan's three generations for the Yuan Dynasty's establishment and consolidation. The forebears of Zhao Shiyan belong to the Yonggu Nationality, so the stele is also called the Ancestral Temple stele of Yonggu. The stele has great value for the study of the calligraphy and history of the Yuan Dynasty.

15. Confucius' Temple

Located in the courtyard of the Government Hostel in East street, The Confucius' temple was constructed in the thirty-eighth year of Wanli (1610 AD) in the Ming Dynasty, first on the eastern mountain of the town seat, then to Xiguan (West Gate), finally to the place where it is now in the thirteenth year of the reign of the Emperor Shunzhi (1656 AD), Qing Dynasty. It was reconstructed several times in the fourth year of the reign of the Emperor Qianlong (1739 AD) and in the nineteenth year of the Emperor of Daoguang (1839 AD).

The magnificent complex of palatial architecture consists of three courtyards and 200 rooms, including Lingxing Gate, Kuixing Garret, Xiangxian Temple and Minghuan Temple. The Palace is just in the center of them. It was occupied by the Government Hostel in 1958 and rebuilt into modern buildings year by year. Today, the temple is protected as a county cultural monument.

16. Red Mountain Garden

Red Mountain, to the east of the town seat, is named for its color. One of the eight ancient scenic spots, it is said that there was a meteorite that is to the east of the town, on which was a long footprint, according to *Lixian Annals*. In 1996, comprehensive administration was carried out, guided by the committee of the Communist Party of China in Lixian and the People's Government of Lixian, now the new buildings and ancient structures, young trees and ancient cypresses set off each other. It is a good place for people to be on holiday or for visiting. The twenty eighth of March till the eighth of April in the Chinese lunar calendar, there is a temple fair, including playing operas and religious homage. The good believers go on a pilgrimage here. The small retailers hawk their small commodities on the both sides of the road. Pleasure and entertainment are the visitors' goals. As a result, there is a thriving and prosperous sight. With the development of Lixian tourism, it will attract more and more visitors in the near future.

17. Stone Tablet of Wang Renyu

This tablet lies in a place named Killing-Dragon Bend in Shiqiao village, to the south of the town seat. Its full name is "a tablet for the teacher of the Crown Prince of Zhou" during the Five Dynasties, and was built for his tomb by his grandson, Wang Yongxi, in the first year of Yongxi (984 AD), Song Dynasty. Lifang composed the inscription on the stone tablet. He was a follower of Wang Renyu, and a prime minister of the Northern Song Dynasty. It was written and cut by Zhanghe. The epitaph recorded and narrated the life of Wang Renyu, a famous politician and writer during the Five Dynasties.

18. New Zhongchuan Martyrs' Mausoleum

Lixian county has a long history. It is an important strategic point and a place contested by all strategists from ancient times. In the Three kingdoms period, Zhuge Liang, the prime minister of Shu Kingdom, went to Qi Mountain personally to send a punitive expedition against Wei Kingdom. His deeds are renowned in history. On the way of the Red Army's Long March, the Second Front Army was divided into three routes, by way of Lixian. The Sixth Army on left Route were led by commander Cheng Baojun, commissar Wang Zheng and Chief of staff Peng Shaohui. They then passed Lüjing, Mawu by way of Tanchang, and arrived at the town of Lixian. By way of four villages as Yacheng, focused in Honghe and engaged in arms expansion and fund raising there. Later, they left Lixian and advanced south to Huixian and Liangdang. Headquarters of the second army of the Middle Route, the Fourth Division of the Second Army, the Thirty-Second Army started off from Lichuan in Mingxian county, by way of Lüjing, and arrived at Shangping. Then, by way of Taoping, Jiangkou, Longlin in the direction of Xihe, Chengxian county. They encountered the enemy Lu Dachang's force, and captured 30 soldiers, 30 guns, and 20 horses. The Sixth Division of the Second Army on the Right Route, led by division commander He Bingyan, commissar Liao Hansheng, started off from Tanchang in the direction of Xihe and Taishi River, but went by way of Quanshui and Baihe villages, so as to confuse the enemy. The Second Front Army of the Red Army operated in Lixian for sixteen days, there were footmarks of theirs left in more than 20 villages\towns. No matter where they went, they disseminated revolutionary principles to the masses, and sowed the seeds of Revolution to awaken the masses

With the first gunshot of China's War of Liberation, the PLA quickly liberated most provinces and areas of China with irresistible force. Not long before Liberation, the last KMT (Kuomintang) magistrate of Lixian, Yan guan, built castles in some places such as Yanguan, Qi Mountain, and drilled holes in the mountain, vainly attempting to echo the 119th Army of the enemy and put up a desperate struggle. A battalion of the 119th Army of the 224th Division was stationed in the wall of Yanguan, guarding the four city gates and went on sentry duty round the clock. In early August in 1949, Tianshui was liberated. The assistant commander of the 58th Rigiment 20th Division 7th Army of the First Field Army, Wang Dingxin, led the liberation army to press on towards Lixian. Keeping abreast of the enemy's situation and depending on the guise of cereal fields in autumn, they rushed out of the wall of Yanguan before the night was out. The first battalion made a detour to Wangcheng from Shangmo, Caotan area, and guarded the west gate. The Second and Third battalion mainly attacked south gate from Sujiacheng to Mapingshan area. At night, they launched a general offensive. Under the circumstance of exhorting and climbing scaling in vain, our liberation army pretended to attack with a small number of troops, assembling massive forces to attack the south gate. The enemy fell into the trap as expected, and the south gate was captured. After fierce fighting, enemy forces surrendered, and the battalion commander of the enemy force Cui Xueli was captured. In this battle, 7 officers and soldiers of the Liberation Army sacrificed their lives (one vice captain, one platoon leader, and five soldiers), a local man was also sacrificed when carrying the wounded. When the battle was over, commander of the Army, Peng Shaohui, commissar Xian Henghan held a victory meeting in the town of Xiaotianshui, cited those who had distinguished themselves in the battle, and buried 8 martyrs who died heroic deaths. A martyrs' mausoleum was also laid out there. In order to praise the glorious achievement of the revolutionary martyrs and study their spirit, the Committee of the Communist Party of China in Lixian erected a monument in the martyrs' park in October 1996, and widened the cemetery site, and built new enclosing walls and fences. This cemetery has now become one of the important patriotic education bases of Lixian.

19. Gaositou Relic

It lies at Gaositou, Shiqiao village, covering 6000 square meters. The culture stories somewhere are 4 meters deep. Many stone-artifacts, potteries, bone-wares have been unearthed for years, the typical one is a Head-shaped Cover, it is one of the representative of the prehistoric portrait shape, the art value is very high. The relics belong to various cultures, such as Yangshao, Qijia and the Zhou Dynasty. It was first discovered by Pei Wenzhong in 1947, and is now protected by the province.

20. Shibeixia Relic

It is located at Shibei village north, Chengguan town. The area is some 30,000 square meters. The culture layer is 0.5—2 meters thick. Pei Wenzhong first discovered a lot of pieces of stone-articles, pottery, bronze-wares in 1947. In the 1970s, people again discovered Bo (a bowl of a kind) in quality in thin mire, red potteries with two or three ears and some stone artifacts. It belongs to the Yangshao and Qijia culture sites.

21. A Cluster of Tombs in Yaoyu

They are located on a pain ground at Yaoyu, Shiqiao village, about

1,000 meters long by 500 meters wide. Several arch tombs of either bricks or soil are opened in the air. They all faced south. The entrance is about 2—2.5 meters. The native farmer discovered more objects when they were constructing the terraced fields. The pottery contain basin, pot, dish, house, well, cooking stove...etc. Bronze articles contain maxian, pike, chu, mirror, wuzhu money etc. They can be judged as a cluster of tombs in the Han Dynasty by the unearthed cultural objects.

22. Chenghuang Temple

It is located at Chenghuang Temple Street. There is no record when it was start to set up. According to the current data, in the forty-sixth year of Wanli(1618 AD), Ming Dynasty, it was rebuilt. And it was maintained many times during the Qing Dynasty. It covers an area of 2,000 square meters. The buildings all face south. There are four palaces, with arrange ments symmetry. The main building contains three palaces and three storied-buildings, covering an area of 45—63 square meters. The mostly parts of construction are wood. The main part was maintained in 1987, it is a representative construction of monastic of the ancient.

23. Red Army Tombs

The tombs are located on the top of East Hill, Longchi village, Caoping town. The Sixth Rigiment of the Second Front Army of the Red Army passed Lixian, on their way from Luojiabu to Honghe, on October seventh 1936. Suddenly, they encountered the air attack and was surrounded by enemy. The model division rushed ahead, Yan Fusheng, commissar of the Sixteenth Division was badly wounded, the medicine unit joined the combat, more than one hundred soldiers sacrificed their lives. At the foot of the hill, a dozen soldiers died and buried right on the spot. There are two clusters of tombs.

Chapter Three   Famous Local Industrial and Agricultural Products

1. Apples

Lixian is also well-known for its excellent apples. Some local species have long been famous all over the country. Especially, Red Marshal, Red Star, Red Crown, The Huaniu apples, which once won a national prize as an excellent agricultural product, are raised at Huaniu village in Tianshui City. Huaniu apples is now a brand, in fact, it means "Three Red Apples". Most of the apple trees are grown here. The different species of apples are widely grown in different places, for its high sugar content, bright color skin, beautiful appearance, and heavy fragrant pulp. They are also suitable for preserving and are liked by people.

2. Bapan Pears

Bapan pears are a speciality of Gansu. The pulp has high water content, yet is crisp and refreshing: they are sweeter than ordinary pears with a rather sour taste. They are noted for their delicious taste and medicinal value. Local people like to eat them boiled or steamed with crystal sugar. Cooked in this way they have good medicinal effects on lung invigoration suppression of coughs, and phlegm reduction.

According to the data, as early as the period of the Reign of Emperor Jiajing, the Ming Dynasty, Lixian started the cultivation of large quantities of Bapan pears. In the 1960s, the arca of planting, as well as the yield reached the highest level in the history. It can be grown on the upper reaches of Xihan River. According to Another legend, Bapan pears once were presented as tribute to the imperial court. In 1996, at the meeting of the whole province fruit-trees technique, Lixian was settled one of the eight Bapan pears production bases.

3. Garlic

Purple and white garlic are both famous products of Lixian. They are remarkable for their large size, plump cloves, and strong flavor. They are excellent for seasoning and as germ-killers. The garlic sprouts have a long stem and bright green color. The garlic stems have a sweet and mild fragrance, juicy and crisp, a pure refreshing taste and high nutritive value.

4. Persimmons

Lixian's persimmons are mainly grown in these places, such as Longlin, Leiba, Wangba. The yearly yield is more than 100,000 kilograms. The main species are Siling persimmon, Shejianghuang, Junqianzhi, etc. The Green persimmons fruit can be used to make persimmons sauce with mulberry leaves or lime solution. They taste sweet and tasty. They are also made Dried persimmons or Wine persimmons. Wine persimmon is again a local special product. First pack the persimmons in the jar after either dipping some white spirit or mixing with the fermented wheat, then seals up the jar completely. Unseal it after few months. The wine persimmons have a yellow or brown color, and have heavy wine taste, delicious and sweet flavor. They are always presented to friends and relatives as delicacy. Both persimmon frost and persimmon roots have medicinal effect.

5. Pomegranates

Lixian pomegranates are primarily divided into 2 species——the white pulp and the red pulp pomegranates. On the white pulp pomegranates, the peel is white, the grain is big, the juice liquid is much, and the flavor is sweet. On the red pulp pomegranates, after they are ripe, they have a bright red color, sweet juice, larger size and best quality. It has a medicinal effect on driving away tapeworms. The fruit peel is wet, and has sour and astringent flavor. It can treat dysentery. They are mainly grown at Pingtou and Yuchi villages in Leiba, Taolin village in Xiaoliang, and yearly yield is more than 500 kilograms.

6. Wild Pepper (Chinese Prickly Ash)

This is one of the famous farming products in Lixian, and is the main source of income of local people as well. Since it is planted for years, the technology of cultivating is very excellent. Some well-known species are grown here, such as, Oily-pepper, which is harvested in June every year; Bright Red Robe, that can be got in either in late June or early July; the Late Weak Pepper that are always harvested in late Autumn.

It is a bush or small arbor of the rue family. Its stem is brown and, has lots of small branches with many plinth, the tender branches are covered with soft hair, the oval leaves are dark green, it bears purplish red fruits with many wart-like and swelling gland dots. No matter when they are ripe, its body will be rent in two, the shining black ball-shaped seeds come out naturally. The rind of it is joined to the base, like a chopped ball. 0.3-0.5 cm in diameter, outside the rind is very coarse with the color from reddish-purple to reddish brown, and some wart-like and swelling oil gland; Inside it is sleek and light yellow. When dried in the sun, it makes a wonderful condiment. Generally speaking, the Oily-pepper is the best wild pepper, which sells at a high price every year. The seeds can either be grown or be made into pepper oil or liquid, both of which are the top grade dressing full of oil, limp and numb, and peppery. It has strong fragrance and lasting hot peppery taste.

The oil dregs can be used as animal feed or fertilizers. The leaves can be eaten, and can be used to defend the insects. The wild pepper bears the drought and is not strict to soil and has very strong adaptability. There are many places in the lower reaches of Xihan River that can be produced, the best ground of the product are Longlin, Leiba, Zhongba, Wangba.

7. Tobacco

Tobacco is grown around the county seat of Lixian, and is high of quality, and far from pollution. When it is dried in the sun, the color is bright golden. It smells fragrant and mild, with preventing insects, mosquito repellent qualities, and general refreshing effects.

The tobacco leaf belongs to the eggplant family, a year-living herb. It is pleased with warm, and bears the drought. The roast tobacco and the basked tobacco may be produced in Lixian. The basked tobacco do not need the deep processing, dried in the sun, then can be smoked directly. Tobacco leaves, particularly, produced at Shengquan village is most famous for its quality.

8. Wangba Tofu

Made from a kind of bean, yellow or black, tofu is very popular in Lixian. The process of making it is very complicated and careful. The soya beans are ground into small pellets first, and the skins of them are blown off, then they are soaked in cold water until they get soft and bigger. A small stone mill turned by hand can grind them into paste. The paste is melted in boiling water and filtered with a piece of emery cloth, over it is beans dregs, the milky water will be cooked. Some salt that is produced in a local place is added to the cooker. Masses of tofu must come out. Just at this time, it is put into a type of square fray, till it gets cold, tofu is made up. It can be served in different ways, cold or hot, fried or boiled. However, tofu is cooked in any means. It contains many vitamins and amino acids, and is high in fat, calories, and nutrients. Being a fragrant, tender and delicious taste, tofu always attracts many people to eat, men or women, old or young.

9. Songhua Honey

Bees make honey in a beehive. It is a refined carbohydrate, semi-transparent and semi-flowing, amber liquid. If we dip a wood stick in it, it will flow down along the stick in a line and form some folded circles. It also has different states in both the hottest and coldest seasons. In summer it is like vegetable oil; in winter it becomes crystal similar to crayon oil with something grain-like. It has a fragrant smell and strong sweet taste. It has peaceful nature benefiting the lungs and the intestines, which is an antipyretic with a moistening, detoxifying function.

10. Malt Sugar with Walnut Kernels

This is a kind of sugar in a traditional method. Let wheat germinate first and the malt is dried in the sun and pounded into pieces. The small corn can be boiled. At this time, put the malt into it, filter and eradicate the dregs. With the big fire, we can mix it with walnut kernels and pour them out. It looks amber and transparent, heated, it will go soft; put it in a cold place, it will become hard. Since walnut kernels have a high oil and protein content, traditional Chinese medicine holds that it is good for nourishing the brain and kidneys and adding luster to hair. The malt and corn are high in sugar and vitamins and have a pure refreshing taste, and high nutritive value.

People who live in Lixian are greatly invigorated after eating such sugar.

11. Walnut

The walnut is an important resource and a volume of value tree in this county. The history of the planting is long. There are Luren walnut, Dama walnut, thin-shell walnut, oil walnut etc. Most are thin-shell walnut: the thin, easily cracked shell opens to reveal a plump, moist, large kernel. It has high oil and protein content. Traditional Chinese medicine holds that it is good for nourishing the brain and kidneys and adding luster to hair, it is also good for eating or oil extraction. It can be grown in Yanhe, Taitang, Zhongba, Baihe, Qiaotou, Wangba, Tanping. Annual output is 180,000 kilograms or so.

12. Imitation Bronzes

It surprised the world when some bronze articles were excavated from the lands of Lixian some years ago, so local people designed and produced replicas of different kinds. They all look much like the original in shape and color. They are boxed for easy shipment and are inexpensive. They are also of high quality and are beautiful red and yellow. They have proven to be excellent as souvenirs and presents. These products are truly works of art worth having.

13. Local Alcoholic beverages

(1) Qinhuang Imperial Spirit.

Qinhuang Imperial Spirit is the new liquor produced by the Lixian Qinhuang Brewery, Which is of recent ingredients. Qinhuang Imperial liquor has a strong fragrance, and looks pure and bright, tastes peculiarly sweet and soft. And it is enjoyed by all.

(2) Minglin Wine.

The wine made in Caoping and Tanping has a distinctive taste with a long history, and is very popular in Lixian. It is made from wheat and corn. It is turbid but has a good taste. Drink after heated. It tastes sweet and mellow but smells only slightly alcoholic. It is refreshing and makes you feel well even when you are drunkard; additional herbal ingredients are sometimes added to.

Chapter Four Wild Vegetables

1. Yangdu Vegetable

Yangdu vegetable, its nickname is Yangdu mushroom. Its name comes from its shape, and it looks like a turning-inside-out sheep's tripe. There are so many kinds of them, such as Heimai Yangdu mushroom, Cutui Yangdu mushroom, Jianding Yangdu mushroom, Little Yangdu mushroom, Gao Yangdu mushroom, Brown Yangdu mushroom, delicious Yangdu mushroom. Yangdu mushroom still has an effect of promoting the human body growth, promoting the hematopoiesis, promoting the immunity. It is also a natural health food for strengthening the body, and increasing intellectual. It costs 1,000 dollars per kilogram or so. It is mainly grown in Sanyu, Wangba, Caoping, Qiaotou, Shajin, Taoping, Luoba, Jiaoshan.

2. Bracken

Bracken is shaped like a hand and so it is also called Buddha's hand (Foshou), but the local name is lucky vegetable. The bracken here is tender green, and grows on some mountains. Since it grows in the wild, bracken is regarded as still free from pollution and people think that it has a special medicinal value for health. It also contains various nutritive minerals and vitamins in abundance.

In China, people started eating bracken long long ago. At first, it only appeared on the common people's dinner table as an ordinary wild herb; later on, it could be found on the tables of high officials and noble lords. It is said that bracken used to be presented as tribute to the imperial court.

When spring comes. The newborn bracken is fresh and very tender, it can be used either for eating right now after washing or being dried and salted. As far as the dried bracken is concerned, for a complex process, the bracken has been boiled with a big fire and hung in a place without sunshine. Finally it is cut into 10 cm long pieces, and put in the sun to dry. Those produced in Lixian have the best color and taste. It has a ready market at home and abroad.

3. Kujie Vegetable

It is another special product, and grows in the wheat or rye fields of the southwest mountain areas in Lixian. It is herb plant, its only stem is strong and upright, the color of leaves is dark green. It bears white flowers and yields black seeds. The seedling can be eaten just after being quickly boiled, and vegetable oil, hot pepper oil and other seasonings are added, it has special aroma and a slightly bitter taste. If it is cut into pieces and salted, it will be golden, good for storage. It has a good taste, fragrant and salty without any bitter taste. Local people like it.

4. Buds of Mulong Tree

This is one of the most popular wild vegetables in Lixian. It is the tender buds of the Mulong tree, which look like thumbs. As they are growing longer, they stretch out naturally. Cook in boiling water and put them into cold water, pour off the water, flash the hotter refined vegetable oil. Mashed garlic and other condiments are added. They have a mild and crisp taste, fragrance with a bit of a medicinal taste.

Chapter Five   Traditional Medicinal Herbs

1. Rhubarb

Rhubarb is a market product of Lixian. It is a kind of herb that grows for years. With the climate being mild and plenty of sunshine and less stored-up water the area of loose black soil, is suitable for it. Rhubarb with palm-like leaves is a perennial herb of the indigo plant family. It is a tall and big herb with deep and resonant roots, a straight stem, which is hollow, round and smooth, and with some hair. There are two kinds of leaves. The ones growing on the roots are big with a long leaf-stem. Outside is sleek and the reverse-side is covered with white hair. The leaves growing on the stem are smaller and bear many small purplish red or light yellow flowers. And bear the triangle brown fruit. It is a main cathartic in Chinese medicinal herb groups. It is used for cleaning the intestine and stomach and tastes bitter with natural cold. The rhubarb seeding is grown from the proved seeds, and transplanted to another field in a random way. Without any organic or chemical fertilizer, they grow up strongly and fast. When they are dug out in August or September, they are thick, juicy stalks that are cooked and eaten like fruit. The main body of the stalk must be cut into three sections, each of which may be given different names. The section of head is called Sujizi, the section of tail is called Shuigenzi and the middle section can be called Dahuang (rhubarb). So they are classified into three grades. Dahuang is certainly the best. After harvesting, they must immediately be smoked dry, or they will go bad. What is more, the longer they are smoked, the better they are. The dried rhubarb has various shapes, such as, round or taper shaped with a dip between two peaks. The rough skin is scraped. It is yellowish brown or reddish brown with whitish reticulated veins or chrysanthemum-like dots. Un-scraped, it is brown. There are some swellings on its surface and cross veins and vertical furrows. The whole light orange section protrudes or is concave everywhere. Rhubarb of good quality is as hard as wood, but loose in the middle and dark brown. It is oily and has a special flavor, a bitter taste with astringent.

2. Milk Vetch

It is a perennial herb of the bean family .The main root is like a long stick with slight wood and is difficult to break. Its skin is red or tawny. The upper straight stalks are lots of outgrowth, smooth or less soft hair. Its seeds are black, kinney shaped. Finished products have a frustum or cylinder shapes. The grayish yellow or light brown bodies have irregular vertical wrinkles or furrows, rough and reliable, with powder character. The section has hair-like strong staple. But the outer layer is loose and light yellow; the center has a special chysanthemum-like veins. It has a rather smell and sweet taste with soya flavor. It enrich vital energy and consolidates the body, eliminates swelling; it is good to the dieresis and skin ulcer.

3. Chinese Thorowax Root

The botany description is: a perennial herb, straight root with little outgrowth is rough. The stalk is growing thickly and straightly with making a bends the letter "Z". The surface of the leaf is green and the reverse side is light green. It bears small, yellow, five petal flowers. The grains are like ellipse. The dried root has tapered shape. The main root is upright and tough. Its skin is grayish brown. The section is wooden fiber, light yellow color, slight fragrance, and has a peppery, bitter taste. It is effective in allaying fever, dredging liver, and raising the vital energy.

4. Licorice

Being a perennial herb, both roots and stem are cylinder-shaped, but the main reddish brown root is very long and wide. The woody stem is upright and covered with short white hairs and scale-like glands. The leaf flake is egg-like with a long stalk. It bears purplish red flowers. The grains are sickle-like or distorted or ring shaped, and covered brown thorn-like gland hair. The seeds are oblate and black. Medicinal licorice is cylinder shaped, brownish red with obvious furrow and ditch veins. When sliced, the section is fiber and sunk in the center with various annular chrysanthemum-like veins. It is substantial and weight, yellowish white and powder character. It has a special fragrance, it has the medicinal properties of invigorating the lung and easing coughs, of enriching the spleen and vital energy, of treating the fever and detoxify, of mediating other medicine.

5. Angelica Root

This is a perennial herb. The stumpy main root is like an irregular cylinder. Its head enlarges a bit and small roots are counted several or more, the straight stalk is purple, small with obvious vertical veins. It often bears white flowers and oval-shaped grains come out from the compound section. The main root can be divided into three parts: The head part is flat and round with leaf-stalk marks and annular lines, this is named Guitou; The middle section is similar to a cylinder with much outgrowth and is called Guishen; The end and outgrowth that is wide in top and thick in the foot most of which is distorted with many small purple hair root marks is named Guiwei. It is pliable and tough. When sliced, it has annular brown veins in the middle and oil dots. It has a special and strong fragrant taste and is rather bitter and peppery.

Danggui produced in Lixian is not as famous as that in Minxian, but it is of high quality and output. It is an effective medicine to enrich the blood, regulate the menstrual cycle, remove blood stasis and promote tissue regeneration. It is an indispensable medicine for the treatment of gynecological diseases.

6. Codonopsis Pilosula

It is one of the volumes of medicine products in this county. There are two kinds of it, the wild-life and the planted. The former growing many years has as the same effect as Baitangshen. Its cortex is rough. The one with a large head is called Lion Head; the one with a chrysanthemum-like gross-grain when sliced is called chrysanthemum heart. Planted codonopsis pilosula contains wendang from Wenxian and white stripe dang from Lintao. The wildlife is grown in the southwest parts of the county. The places with the cultivation of this herb are Taoping and Baiguan.

Chapter Six   Local Snacks

The cuisine is a distinctive part of Chinese Civilization. Although there are fewer varieties of food in Lixian than in other parts, it has its own typical dishes and refreshments. With its important location and long history, the local snacks, however, originated from this place or imported from other places, all, are especially appetizing. They are a pleasure not to be denied during a visit to Lixian.

1. Hot Starch Noodles

The starch is washed out of the flour in a sticky state. The water starch is put into special shallow steamers usually made of galvanized iron or aluminum, for cooking. The cooked mianpi is cut into small pieces, like noodles when it isn't getting cold, then mixed with several pieces of steamed gluten of which the substance left over is made and hot pepper oil (pungent sauce), mashed garlic, vinegar, other dressings to taste. Heavily seasoned, but not too greasy, it has a long lasting after-taste. Local people are never tired of it. If it gets cold, it is semi-transparent, as smooth as jelly, pliable and tough as noodles.

2. Lard Cakes

Dough is mixed with lard, and is fried into golden brown cakes. The cakes are fragrant, moist and delicious. But the paste takes a lot of skill to make. Most of local people are good at it. Sometimes eggs are used as the filling for the paste. Cakes of this kind are called Egg-Lard cakes. They are good snacks all year round and enjoyed by all.

3. Buckwheat Heluo Noodles

These are another Lixian snack. The process is an ancient and difficult one. The buckwheat must be ground into flour first. Chopping the dough into slices and making the Heluo noodles requires special equipment. They can be eaten cold or with various Saozi soups. They are delicious and very popular. They are a good summertime snack for people, especially women.

4. Saozi Noodles

Cooked wheaten food is the staple for the local people. For many years, they have developed many ways to cook it. Saozi noodles, both handmade and machine-made, are one of the best known. As far as the handmade ones are concerned, cutting noodles is quite an art. The dough is rolled as thin as paper and sliced as fine as thread. The soup ingredients may be meat or eggs or vegetables, they taste spicy, hot, or sour, but ingredients are fresh, local products. Each family likes to make its own. When a thick soup made of pork and dainties of any kind is poured into the prepared noodles. They make a delicious feast.

5. Unleavened Bread with Pork

Pork is stewed with salty water, honey juice and other seasonings. It is often heated on a stove. When eaten, the pork is taken out of the cooker and cut into very small pieces, then the unleavened bread can also be cut into halves, and the pork is put in it. At last some meat soup is poured onto it, too. If you are anxious about tasting, hold it with your hand. Of course, cooked in this way, the soup is fragrant and rich with strong tastes. The pork is fresh and tender but not heavy; the bread is crisp and delicious. Local people have it for breakfast every morning.

6. Sweet Fermented Wheat

This is a good summertime snack. Fermented wheat is kept in a big basin. Cold, boiled water and sugar are added to some fermented wheat. It is cool, refreshing, antipyretic and thirst quenching.

7. Kuanchuan Jelly

Cold Jelly is sold all over the county. It is made of buckwheat. First buckwheat is ground into flour. Get rid of the skin and make it into rough, then wash in cool water. The water can be put in a cook and special equipment to mix. Heat with a slow fire until it becomes a mass and cool it. Cut it into cubes and put in a large bowl containing a little vegetable oil, pepper oil. And mashed garlic, sesame oil, vinegar and other dressing are added. It's a good snack in summer.

8. Various Baked or Roast Delicacy

Most of these delicious snacks can be found on the street on any evening. Such as roast mutton on skewers roast fish, roast chicken, even roast potatoes, and so on. No matter what is roasted over a charcoal fire and seasoned with different condiments, it will have a unique taste, tender, fresh and crisp, and will attract more and more passers-by to taste. For instance, mutton shashlik, the mutton is roasted on a quick fire, heavily seasoned with three peppers, including ground red hot pepper, Chinese prickly ash (wild pepper), pepper, and salt. It tastes short and fresh but not greasy, rare and without the strong smell usually associated with it.

9. Yanguan Dumplings

Yanguan Dumplings is a typical local snack. First of all, make the flour into dough, and to thin slice by handicraft or machine, carve into small square pieces, put the seasoned fillings, make it in different shapes by hand. Before eaten, it must be cooked in the boiling water. The fillings can be made of dried-egg with Chinese chives, tofu with shallots, dried-potatoes with Chinese chives, even lean pork or mutton. While it is eaten, all kinds of soup can also be added. Its characteristics: the fillings are delicious and refreshing, the outside skin is crisp and fragrant. It has a long aftertaste.

10. Yongxing Pulled Noodles

Add the proper amount of ash powder or salt to wheat flour, and make it into the regiment, then divide the dough into an-inch-long section. Daub the surface with vegetable oil, preventing to glue or to become mutually hard. Open it with a small noodle-stick, both the ends are held tightly and pulled by hand, after several times, it will become stripe-like, then cook in the boiling water. While eaten, some soups might be added according to the different taste. Yongxing pulled noodles, slippery in tasty, and bright in color, is deeply liked by Lixian people.

Chapter Seven   Supplementary Reading

1. A Rare Kind of Fish——Giant Salamander

This rare and valuable fish is abounding in the brooks in the mountains. It is a less-scale fish, with flat body, gray dorsal, and light white belly. It looks like a bare personal body. There is a head, a neck and four limbs with five fingers or toes. It is of great medicinal value, which can mend the bone and regenerate muscle that is also called "Jiegudan" in this area.

2. Examination of Lixian County's Name

Lixian county's name comes from the name of a place. Changdao county, from the Sui and Tang Dynasties to the Song Dynasty, was established in Lijiadian (now known as Dian-zi), 15 kilometers away from the east of today's county seat.

During the Yuan Dynasty, Changdao county was put into the Xihe State, Li-dian was set up in today's Chengguan town. The Headquarters of the Mongolian and Han armies in Wenzhou. As a result, It is quite close from Changdao county, also called "Li-dian Fu".

When the Confucian scholars felt that the word "Li" was not elegant, they got another word "Li" to replace it, which formed the mixed use of "Li" and "Li" in the Yuan Dynasty. It can be proved that "Li-dian" was written in the history of the Yuan Dynasty.

3. Lixian County Seat

Lixian county seat is Chengguan town, which located in the middle of the county, the intersection of the Xihan River and the Swallow River, the center of town is in the east longitude 105 degrees, 34 degrees north latitude. 1,403.8 meters above sea level, 97 kilometers east from Tianshui, 250 kilometers south to Wudu, 345 kilometers north to the provincial capital Lanzhou. The town is the county's political, economic, cultural and transportation center.

Lixian county develops very early, During the Zhou Dynasty, it was the birthplace of the Qin people, During the Qin and Han Dynasties, it belonged to the Xixian county, and during the Northern and Southern Dynasties, it was divided into Lancang, Hanyang. From the Sui and Tang Dynasties to the Song Dynasty, It was called Changdao, Tanshui, Datan and so on. During the Yuan Dynasty, the military and civilian governor's office was established in today's county seat. In the early Ming Dynasty, a military and civil organ of local power was established. In the ninth year of Chenghua (1473 AD) of the Ming Dynasty, The parts of the Qin state was made up of Lixian county. The seat was enlarged on the west, and the city walls were built on the south, north and west, and the county town was built. The east wall of the county is the west wall of the city. The west gate of the city was called Chuancheng gate. During the reign of Emperor Shunzhi of the Qing Dynasty, the county seat was seated. During the Qing Dynasty and the period of the Republic of China, the walls were refitted. In the 18th year of the Republic of China (1929 AD), the county began to take shape, and was basically completed. The wall was over 1.5 kilometers in circumference and 10 meters high. It had four towers, a sentry tower, eight forts, and barracks. The town has four main streets, and equipped with Hongxue street, Guangfeng street, Quxiang, Xuejia street, Huangmiao street, Chusi lane, Liujia street, Lujia street, Sanduo street, Cangyuanhou street, Jihou street, Panjia street, Xuexiang, all up to 13 alley.

In the 30th year of the Republic of China (1941 AD) Lixian county began to set up a town, which was called "Tianjia town", and it was renamed Chengguan town in 1952. Chengguan town commune was established in 1958, and restored to Chengguan town in 1983. After the expansion in 1990 and the construction of small towns in 2000, today's county with many buildings, spacious streets, and prosperous roads, is becoimg a modern town.

4. Sites of Heaven Worship in the Han Dynasty

The project of "exploring the origin of Qin people", which has attracted the attention of all circles at home and abroad, will continue. The relevant departments of Gansu province are planning to carry out the "early Qin culture research project of the south east Gansu". During a half-year field survey in 2004, archaeologists found a large site, which is now tentatively identified as a massive Han Dynasty Heaven Worship site.

Since March 2004, the Institute of Cultural Relics and Archaeology of Gansu province, Shaanxi province, the National Museum of China, the Institute of Archaeology of Beijing University, and the Department of Archaeology of Northwest Normal University jointly established a research group and a joint expedition team of the early Qin culture, under the support, participation and cooperation of Lixian county museum, the 6-year-project of "the early capital and mausoleum of Qin and early Qin culture research and excavation" was implemented.

The survey started from March 28, 2004, the team conducted a comprehensive survey of the Xihan River and its tributaries. During this survey, all kinds of 98 sites were discovered.Compared with the 1950s, there are over 70 newfound sites more than before.

5. The Ancient Eight Scenes in Lixian County

(1) God's Feet of Chitu: in Chitu mountain.

(2) God Spring and Ancient Hole: in Guquan village.
(3) Holy Spring Night Moon: in Shengquan village.
(4) Sound of Wind Blowing Pine: in Cuifeng hill.
(5) Mist up the Luanting Mountain: in Shuiwan village.
(6) Tianjia Rich Beautiful Plot: in Chengguan town.
(7) Qi Mountain Twilight Rain: in Qi Mountain village.
(8) Leifeng Sunset: in Leiwang township.

6. Folklore

(1) Washing mind with the river water.

Wang Renyu, was a famous poet in The Five Dynasties with 385 poems. When he was young, his family was poor. He was making a living with chopping woods. At the age of 20, he was still illiterate.

One day, he wandered along Xijiang River and he was falling asleep on a large stone outside some Temple, he dreamt a terrible dream. He came up to the bank and looked at himself surprisingly in the water, a bad-looking young man, with dragged clothes and appeared in front of him. Suddenly there came a big man, with a red face and a white beard, a big knife in his hand. The man put him down on ground, and cut his stomach open, picked down his heart, and washed it in the river, there came out a lot of smell. The man put it into his belly cavity again after a while. Wang Renyu was too frightened to say a word. Just a moment, he smelt a wonderful smell, he opened his eyes to see, there was piles of golden sand with a nice fragrance. He put up the sand with his hands and swollen it down. Only a minute there was nothing on there. Wang Renyu felt very surprised when there came out a giant in the river, thus made him cry out and full down from the stone.

From then on, Wang Renyu became nice and wise and very interested in books. While he was reading, he always remembered everything; while he was composing, he always made a good works. People said it was the water that washed his mind.

(2) Zhuge Liang planted grass.

It is said Zhuge Liang led troops to Qi Mountain, when his troops was beaten, he learnt a lesson from failure, one of the important reason was the supply, so he made his mind to planted grass.

One night, Zhuge Liang decided to order Zhang Bao to search for a experienced shepherd who could teach them how to plant grass. The next day, Zhuge Liang was talking with troops when a noise came up to his ears. When he came out to see, he found that dozens of horses tied to the mellows, which were strong and fat, Zhang Bao was talking with an old man who had white beard and hair. It was original that Zhang Bao and his troops hid on the road in the early morning, when they met, the old man and his fellows mistook them robbers. They fought and made noises. Zhuge Liang apologized to the old man and told his idea to him. The old man introduced Zhuge Liang purple flower clover. A few days later, Zhuge Liang himself came to Quanmagou to visit the old man, and he told Zhuge Liang his family history. He belonged to Ma Chao, who was the son of the leader of West Liang. he was beaten by Cao Cao and gave in Liu Bei. He has been living with his grandson after wounded in the field of battle, led a dog life, gathering the wild fruits and keeping horses.

The old man gave all the seeds of clovers to Zhuge Liang. Zhuge Liang appointed him leader, who was in charge of growing the grass—clover. The soldiers made up as local people, tried to grow clover along Wei River, from the foot of Qi Mountain to the top of it. Zhuge Liang himself grew some on the hillside on the south of Wei River, which is still kept by the local people.

When Wei troops leant that zhuge Liang had planted grass in order to defend, they attacked Qi Mountain. Qi Mountain was occupied, when the soldier of Shu retreated, the old man was planting the clover in the south mountain. Zhang Bao was in charge of cover, and urged the old man to walk quickly. However the man took over the drumstick, push Zhang Bao to go. He did not leave until the clover was all grown and the last soldier left. He himself was shot to die by Wei's soldier disorderly arrows. Up to now, this place is called Lei Gu Ping by the local people.

(3) The origin of "Leifeng Sunset".

Leiwang's temple is located in Leiwang township, which is to commemorate Lei Wangbao who has done a lot of good things such as diagnosis and treatment of disease, and drought relief. Once a few literati scholars came to visit Leiwang's temple. When they came out of the gate, the sun was shining brightly. They looked back and saw the hall of Leiwang's temple on the top of the mountain. So they named it "Leifeng Sunset", from then on "Leifeng Sunset" with its unique charm as one of the eight ancient Lixian county scenery.

Legend has it that in the first year of Kaiyuan in Tang Dynasty, The Emperor was ill, and the imperial doctors could not treat him. At this time, a native official, come from Longshang, said that there was a doctor called Lei Wangbao lived in the eastern part of Qinzhou, who had a great deal of experience, and with the art of heaven, could treat the Emperor's disease. Lei Wangbao was declared into the palace, with his extraordinary skill, the illness was cured. The Emperor was overjoyed and decided to keep Lei Wangbao in his palace. Otherwise, Lei Wangbao determined to cure disease for the people at the beginning of learning the medical, of course, he refused to stay in the palace for the Emperor. The Emperor finally approved. When he left, the Emperor named him "Cover the sky, Cover the ground, Cover the country Leiwang". After Lei Wangbao said thanks, before the Emperor changed his mind, he quickly left for his hometown.

After Lei Wangbao left, there was a minister told the Emperor: "Lei Wangbao's honor is too big, 'Cover the sky, Cover the ground, Cover the country Leiwang' this might even covered the Emperor yourself." The Emperor listened, and just wake up, hurriedly he ordered General Ji and General Zhao to chase Lei Wangbao, and secretly ordered where he was caught up, where to be killed.

Lei Wangbao reached Taihuang mountain(also called Leiwang mountain), he predicted that someone was chasing him, quickly broadcast a handful of rapeseeds (this place is now known as Caizipo), quickly a piece of greenly vegetable covered all over the moment. General Ji and General Zhao was stopped by it. Lei Wang walked to a big bay, looking back, General Ji and General Zhao nearly caught up, he sew thorn seeds (this place is now known as thorn bay), the thorn suddenly grown up, General Ji and General Zhao could not advance, they took the blade to cut them. Finally they made a way to catch up. when they got to a slope, Lei Wangbao spread a handful of sand, suddenly the wind blown from everywhere, with sand and small stone (this place is now known as the Sand slope), The heavy sand stopped General Ji and General Zhao, they could not move forward. Their horses struggled out with difficulties, but Lei Wangbao had disappeared. They hurried to chase Lei Wangbao, and Lei Wangbao threw a handful of tarragon seeds behind him. In the blink of an eye, tarragon grew as deep as a man. Because of the barrier of tarragon, Leiwang just ran up Taihuang mountain. Suddenly he saw a big ditch in front of him. He was about to escape, but General Ji and General Zhao were coming, Lei Wangbao was nasty, and spread a handful of bamboo seeds, instantly bamboo grew and became a forest. The ditch was sealed, Lei Wangbao got out of the ditch, suddenly listened the shouting again. He hastily spread the last handful of burr seeds he had with him in the air (this place is now known as burr bay) and turned to run. he came to a ridge, the ridge was very high, General Ji and General Zhao immediately arrived, Lei Wangbao was anxious, and he took a blade to cut the ridge into two sections (this place is now known as broken strings) General Ji and General Zhao did not rein in the horse. Lei Wangbao shouted to them "you want to die or want to live?" They beg for mercy, but Lei Wangbao turned over the blade, they fell down into the deep stream. After they died, their soul went to heaven, the local people still call them "Master Ji and Master Zhao". Their bodies were buried on the spot.

  Lei Wangbao no longer planned to go home, he knew that the Emperor would hunt him, he lived in Taihuang mountain, alchemy cultivation (this place is now known as the cave cliff, alchemy hole is still in), collected 100 medicine for the local people diagnosis and treatment of disease. the place where Lei Wangbao sunned the herbs was still in, people call it "sunning herbs field."

Taihuang mountain has been called Leiwang mountain ever since.

7. News Report

The Xihan River to Sing the Ancient Hero Song, the Qin Culture to Rewrite a New Chapter
——Amazing Discovery of the Qinshihuang's Hometown
Pang Shidong

Lixian county is an ancient and magical place, which is a greenhouse for brilliant future and great achievements. The sites of prehistoric culture, the pre-Qin culture and the Three Kingdoms culture are scattered all over the area. Located in the east of the county, near the mountains and waters, the Dabuzi mountain is embedded as a bright pearl in this land. With the gradual progress of the national archaeological work, the newly discovered and excavated sites, sacrificial pits, bronze Bianzhong and other archaeological achievements have made this "pearl" even more dazzling, attracting the attention of the world and shocking both at home and abroad.

According to textual research, there were four mausoleum areas during the Qin Dynasty, the second, third and fourth mausoleum areas were successively confirmed before 1987, namely Yongcheng mausoleum area (west mausoleum), Zhiyang mausoleum area (east mausoleum) and the Qinshihuang mausoleum area in Shaanxi province. But the location of the first mausoleum area has always been a mystery to historians and archaeologists. In 1993, in Dabuzi mountain area of Yongxing town, Lixian county, two tombs of Qin's aristocracy were discovered. Through the domestic research of archaeology and history experts, this area was identified as one of four mausoleum areas of the Qin Dynasty, namely "Qin Xichui mausoleum", with an area of 18 square kilometers. This mausoleum includes 14 tombs, 2 holes with ancient chariot and horses.300 pieces of cultural relics were unearthed, including Ding, Gui, Hu and other large bronze ritual vessels and vessels of gold, etc. Among them, two tombs are grand, the total length is 88 meters and 115 meters respectively. Through the expert research, it was preliminarily confirmed that the mausoleum might be the Qin xianggong couple's or their son and daughter-in-law Qin wengong couple's mausoleum. Therefore, it was determined as the mausoleum of Qingong by the historians, which caused a sensation at home and abroad, thus revealing a great mystery in the history and archaeology circles of China and the world for thousands of years. Through archaeology, excavation and research, the ancient tombs discoverd on Dabuzi mountain in Lixian county were confirmed as "Xiquanqiu (Xichui) mausoleum" by experts. They also identified it as the first mausoleum of the ancestors of the first emperor of the Qin Dynasty. Some expert thought that the discovery is one of the greatest excavations in 20th century following the Dunhuang and the Terra Cotta Warriors. The study of pre-Qin period's politics. economy, military, culture, metallurgy, casting, ritual and mausoleum system has immeasurable historical value and academic value, which would fill in the blank of the research of the pre-Qin culture. Professor Gao Chongwen, Director of the Department of Archaeology at Peking University, said: "This is an important breakthrough in the archaeology of the pre-Qin culture. More importantly, the discovery in Lixian county will surely reveal the mystery of the ruins of early capital of Qin."

In recent ten years, the county party committee and county government of Lixian, with the support from provincial and municipal governments as well as the national, provincial administration of cultural heritage, aming at the protection and utilization of Qingong mausoleum, made unremitting efforts. The "National Qin People Xichui Culture Symposium" was held, and also the Arthur M.Sackler Museum of Art and Archaeology at Peking University held the "Xichui Mausoleum Bronze Exhibition of Lixian County, Gansu Province", which made the reputation of Qingong mausoleum known by the world. In 1997, the people's government of Gansu province listed Dabuzi mountain Qingong mausoleum in Lixian county as a key cultural relic protection unit of the whole province, and announced the scope of protection of Dabuzi mountain Qingong's mausoleum. In July 2001, the mausoleum was officially listed by the State Council as the fifth batch of national cultural relics protection units. For a better protection and exploitation and utilization of the site, in 2002, the county has entrusted the Ancient Architecture Design and Research Institute of Shaanxi Province to draw up a plan for the protection of Qingong mausoleum site. At the same time, Lixian county invited archaelogy and architectural experts of Shaanxi, Gansu provinces to the "Symposium of Dabuzi Mountain Sites and Mausoleum Protection Planning". This indicated that in the near future, the early Qin culture, such as the capital, residence, architecture, casting, ritual and mausoleum, will be vividly displayed in front of the world.

Early Qin culture research is a systematic project.The workload is heavy and wide. In the support from the state and provincial administration of cultural heritage, in March 2004, the Institute of Cultural Relics and Archaeology of Gansu province, Shaanxi province, the National Museum of China, the Institute of Archaeology of Beijing University, and the Department of Archaeology of Northwest Normal University jointly established a research group and a joint expedition team of the early Qin culture. They made a plan to conduct a comprehensive survey of the Xihan River and its tributaries in five years.

According to documents, the water basin of the Xihan River was the central area for the early activities of the Qin people, which was confirmed by the discovery of the tomb of Qingong. The joint archaeological team firstly focused on the Xihan River basin. Archaeological team started from Tianshui in the east, to Lixian county in the west,and they conducted a systematic survey about 40-kilometer long Xihan River water on both sides of the area and the tributaries, 10 professional researchers were divided into 2 groups, through 3-year hardworking and investigation,the archaeological work of the early Qin culture had made a big progress, which once again shocked both at home and abroad.

Wang Hui, the deputy director of the Gansu provincial Institute of

Cultural Relics and Archaeology, said that a large number of sites related to the Qin people during the Zhou and Qin Dynasties have been discovered through the investigation of the Xihan River and its tributaries in Lixian county. A total of 98 sites of various types were discovered, including more than 70 new sites. Among the 47 sites of Zhou Dynasty, 38 were dominated by Qin culture, and the "Liubatu—Feijiazhuang" "Dabuzi—Zhaoping" "Leishen temple (Xishan)—Shigouping" were three relatively independent and connected sites, which could be the three central areas of activities of the early Qin people. The archaeological investigation of the water basin in Xihan River provides important clues for exploring some outstanding issues in history, such as the "Xiquanqiu" in the early capital of the Qin Dynasty, the formation of Qin culture, and the relationship between Qin and Rong. At the same time, the archaeological team also found three sites from the Zhou Dynasty to the Spring and Autumn Period in the Xishan mountain, Dabuzi mountain and Shanping county. The site of the Xishan mountain was built along the mountain. The sections of the city wall have been found with a total length of about 1,200 meters. The abandonment date is no later than the early Spring and Autumn Period. At the same time, 800 tombs were found, as well as the ruins of housing base, ash pit, ancient road, kiln, etc. The archaeological team basically understood the scope, structure and layout of Xishan ruins and urban sites.

  The discovery of the sacrificial sites in Luanting mountain in the west of the county is another important achievement in the archaeological work of early Qin culture. The site consists of a sacrificial altar at the top of Luanting mountain with an elevation of 1,700 meters and rammed earth platforms on the mountainside. Nearby the sacrificial pits of the Zhou Dynasty and more than 80 tombs of the Warring States Period were found. The team unearthed sacrificial jade, Wadang and animal bones, which proved that the site in the Zhou Dynasty had human habitation and activities. In a shallow half-moon shaped ditch about 20 meters long from east to west in the Han Dynasty, 11 sets of integrated jade articles were cleaned out, including 51 pieces of Gui, Bi and Jade Doll. The largest diameter of Gui is about 15 cm long and 10 cm wide. The largest diameter of Bi is about 22 centimeters. Gui was made of sapphire, Bi was made of white jade. there were two Jade Doll, they looked like a man and a woman. They were unearthed together. This site should be a special place for heaven worship in the Han Dynasty, which provides important materials for studying the jade used in sacrificial ceremony and related rites in the Han Dynasty.

In recent years, through investigation, people found the distribution of Dabuzi mountain site, Shanping site and the dome hill, Yantuya two noble cemetery within 10 square kilometers. The total area of Dabuzi mountain site is more than 500,000 square meters. In addition to a small number of Qijia cultural relics, the main body is the city site, mausoleum and residence site outside the city, small and medium-sized cemetery outside the east city, Qingong Tomb and sacrificial pit in the central area and the other parts in the Zhou Dynasty. The site was built on a hillside and the plane was roughly rectangular, with rammed earth walls, and the east and west walls were 1,000 meters long. The north wall was about 250 meters long, while the south wall had not been found. The site covers an area of about 250,000 square meters, including the tomb of Qingong, the site of fire-shaped buildings and sacrificial pits. The site inside and outside the city has drilled 1.29 million square meters. So far, a total of 699 sites have been found, including rammed earth walls, building sites, ash pits, pottery kilns, tombs, Wells and the pits of horses and chariots. In 2006, the largest building site was unearthed in Dabuzi mountain site, which is 102 meters long, 17 meters wide. The building base was surrounded by rammed earth walls, there were 17 large stone bases. The west wall remnants were about 20 to 60 cm high above the ground and 1.5 meters wide, while the underground foundation was about 3 meters wide. The east, north and south wall only remained the foundation part, which was about 2 to 3 meters wide. The scale of the building is large, as a large palace type of architecture. From the accumulation of strata and the inclusion of rammed earth, the foundation of the building was built around the late Western Zhou Dynasty and the early Spring and Autumn Period, abandoned during the Warring States Period and seriously damaged during the Han Dynasty. The upper part of the east wall was completely destroyed due to the terraced ground construction. Six tombs, one chariot and horse pit, four human sacrificial pits and four utensils pits have been excavated. The newly excavated worship pit, which might have been used to worship the God of the earth. The most eye-catching cultural relic unearthed in this excavation was a set of bronze chimes in the early Qin Dynasty, which were composed of 3 big bells and 8 small ones. The appearance was complete and the whole is dark green. Archaeologists said that the set of chimes was so well preserved when they were completely unearthed, they could still play wonderful music again.

Through this investigation, drilling and excavation, the team basicly understood the layout and structure of the site. The excavation of Dabuzi mountain site found a large palace structure with rammed earth wall and a base as well as the sacrificial pits excavated a set of bronze bells, which provided extremely precious materials for understanding the nature of Dabuzi site, confirming the owner of the Qingong tomb and studying the sacrificial rites, the rites and music system and bronze casting technology at that time. At the same time, it also provided a scientific basis for the protection and utilization of Dabuzi mountain ruins.

A number of national treasures such as the Zhou Dynasty city sites and residence sites, the tombs outside the city, the sacrificial pits and bronze bells unearthed at the Dabuzishan site are from the western Zhou Dynasty to the Spring and Autumn Period. Its size is rare. According to *The Historical Record Of Qin* written by Sima Qian, the people of Qin were mainly active in the southeast of present-day Gansu during the Western Zhou Dynasty, while the capital city "Xiquanqiu" (Xichui) and the mausoleum of the ancestors of Qin were located in the upper reaches of the Xihan River in present Lixian county. This proved that the record of Sima Qian is credible. At the same time, this excavation revealed for the first time the remains of large-scale settlement of early Qin people, and obtains new information for understanding the living pattern of Qin people at that time. Through the discovery of a large number of remains related to the Qin people during the

Zhou and Qin Dynasties, it is further proved that Lixian county was the center of activities of the early Qin people and the seat of Xixian county during the Qin and Han Dynasties. It is the true birthplace of Qin culture and the ancestor of Qin Dynasty.

The archaeological project of early Qin culture is a major cultural project in the new century. Lixian county is one of the birthplaces of the Chinese nation with a long history, numerous historical sites, rich and unique regional cultural heritage. It is reasonable to believe that in the future archaeological excavations, the joint archaeological team will have more unexpected harvest, and the "historical memory" will shock the world again.

From *Longnan Daily*, November 25, 2006, weekend special issue

参考文献　References

[1] 礼县志编纂委员会. 礼县志[M]. 西安：陕西人民出版社，1999.
[2] 马建营. 秦西垂史地考述[M]. 兰州：敦煌文艺出版社，2010.
[3] 周德祥，张克复. 礼县史话[M]. 兰州：甘肃文化出版社，2011.